AUG - - 2013

Birds & blooms gardening for birds
butterflies.
635.96 BIR

P9-CTP-323

BIRDS & BLOOMS

GARDENING

for birds & butterflies

BIRDS&BLOOMS
Gardening for Birds & Butterflies

Vice President, Editor-in-Chief Catherine Cassidy
Vice President, Executive Editor/Books Heidi Reuter Lloyd
Senior Editor/Books Mark Hagen
Associate Creative Director Edwin Robles Jr.
Associate Editor/Books Ellie Martin Cliffe
Project Art Director Angie Packer
Layout Designer Catherine Fletcher

Copy Chief Deb Warlaumont Mulvey
Copy Editor Joanne Weintraub
Contributing Proofreader Jean Dal Porto
Photo Coordinator Trudi Bellin
Assistant Photo Coordinator Mary Ann Koebernik
Horticulture Experts Melinda Myers, Sally Roth
Birding Expert George Harrison
Butterfly Experts Tom Allen, Kenn Kaufman
Contributors Alison Auth, Kris Drake, Beth Evans-Ramos, Bill Johnson,
Lenora Larsen, Jennifer Mancier, Mike Matthews, David Mizejewski,
Anne Schmauss, David Shaw, Daisy Siskin, Lisa Szczygiel-Durante,
Kris Wetherbee, Ann Wilson

Executive Editor/Home & Garden Heather Lamb
Creative Director/Home & Garden Sharon K. Nelson
Editor/Birds & Blooms Stacy Tornio
North American Chief Marketing Officer Lisa Karpinski
Vice President/Book Marketing Dan Fink
Creative Director/Creative Marketing Jim Palmen

The Reader's Digest Association, Inc.
President and Chief Executive Officer Robert E. Guth
Executive Vice President, RDA, and President, North America Dan Lagani

©2012 Reiman Media Group, LLC
5400 S. 60th St., Greendale WI 53129-1404
All rights reserved. Printed in USA.

International Standard Book Number (10): 1-61765-002-1
International Standard Book Number (13): 978-1-61765-002-4
Library of Congress Control Number: 2011938023

On the Cover: Bluebird: Bill Leaman
Monarch: Don Johnston / All Canada Photos / Corbis
For more, visit *birdsandblooms.com*

FRANKLIN TOWNSHIP PUBLIC LIBRARY
485 DEMOTT LANE
SOMERSET, NJ 08873
732-873-8700

I always feel a sense of appreciation—and even a bit of wonder—when I see a songbird exploring my backyard. While wildlife gardeners like me enjoy cultivating our flowers and veggies, it's when we can share the experience with local birds and butterflies that we feel most fulfilled. Nature is just that amazing.

In *Gardening for Birds & Butterflies*, the *Birds & Blooms* editors have collaborated with our magazine's experts to show you how easy yet rewarding wildlife gardening can be—from creating seasonal havens for a variety of creatures to planting the flowers, trees and shrubs your favorite fliers can't resist. Plus, in our bonus gardener's field guides, you'll learn about North America's best-loved birds and butterflies—more than 100 species in all.

But what makes this valuable resource truly special is that it's chock-full of contributions from gardeners and birders like you! Scattered throughout the pages, you'll find surefire tips, clever projects and gorgeous photos from folks across the U.S. and Canada who share a love of wildlife gardening.

Why don't you join us?

Happy gardening!

Stacy Tornio

Stacy Tornio
Editor, *Birds & Blooms*

creature key
Want to know what types of wildlife are attracted to certain flowers, trees and shrubs? Watch for these symbols in plant profiles throughout the book:

 attracts birds   attracts butterflies

table of CONTENTS

6 Welcoming Wildlife

8 **Birdscaping Made Easy** Make your backyard irresistible to friendly fliers with just a couple of simple tricks.

12 **Go Native!** Bring in more birds and butterflies by including native plants in your landscape.

14 **Wildlife Landscaper Q&A** Four garden designers share their top secrets.

16 **Pacific Paradise** This gardener transformed a hillside retreat into a wildlife haven.

20 **Backyard Wilderness** From a large pond to native plants, this reader's garden is an oasis for wildlife.

22 **Field of Dreams** See why this Detroit transplant learned to love Kansas soil.

24 Wake up to Spring

26 **Spring Backyard Checklist** Get an early start with these seasonal to-do's.

28 **Butterfly Gardening on a Budget** Attract flying flowers without spending a fortune on plants.

30 **Out on a Limb** No matter the species, each hummingbird's nest is one-of-a-kind artwork.

32 **30 Plants for a Stellar Spring Garden** Transform your yard with fliers in mind.

38 **Glorious Spring Wildlife Gardens** Start the year right with one of these planting plans.

40 **Stunning Spring Containers** Perk up any space with a blend of potted blooms.

44 **Spring Birding Basics** Bring more of them to your yard with our seasonal pointers.

46 **Year-Round Butterflies: Spring** Keep an eye out for these early fliers.

47 **Glad You Asked** Our resident experts welcome your springtime wildlife-garden questions.

49 **Backyard Builders** Get inspired by these clever birders who gave their old junk new life.

50 **Bluebird B&B** This unique nesting box doubles as a mealworm feeder.

52 **Orange Wreath for Orioles** Simple and elegant, these little feeders will bring in oodles of fliers.

53 **Cup & Saucer Feeder** Schedule a coffee date with your backyard birds.

54 **Spring Garden Gallery** Watch the world awaken through the eyes of shutterbugs.

56 Soaking in Summer

58 **Summer Backyard Checklist** Tackle these simple chores so you can spend more time savoring your bird and butterfly paradise!

60 **Backyard Color Guide** Learn which hues will attract wildlife to your garden.

62 **Beyond Butterflies** Lay out the welcome mat for the helpful insects in your yard.

66 **Summer Plants Birds & Butterflies Love** Count on these flowers, trees and shrubs to entice friendly fliers.

76 **Warm-Weather Gardens for Birds & Butterflies** Heat up summer in your backyard with one (or more!) of these wildlife magnets.

80 **Sizzling Summer Containers** Designate hot spots for friendly fliers with a floral creation.

84 **Summer Birding Basics** You'll see plenty of activity at feeders and birdbaths now.

86 **Year-Round Butterflies: Summer** This time of year, flying jewels are everywhere.

87 **Glad You Asked** Make your backyard a mini wildlife sanctuary with our experts' solutions.

89 **Backyard Builders** Celebrate summer by displaying a beachy birdhouse like these.

90 **Let's Go Batty** Insect-eating predators play a valuable role in maintaining a healthy backyard.

92 **Feeder in a Jar** Turn a recycled baby food jar into a pretty, practical hummingbird feeder.

93 **Pint-Sized Pond** All you need is a barrel to create a tiny pool of serenity.

94 **Summer Garden Gallery** Keep your mind off the season's sweltering temps with these cool summertime photos.

96 In Awe of Autumn

98 Fall Backyard Checklist Work your way through this quick list, and you'll be spotting more birds and butterflies than ever.

100 Food for Flight Give migratory birds the flying fuel they need.

104 The Magic of Maples Ornamental trees offer much more than a bit of shade.

106 Attract More Birds & Butterflies This Fall These plants are irresistible to autumn wildlife.

112 Fall Gardens for Birds & Butterflies Welcome late-season fliers with a fuss-free planting plan.

114 Perfect Fall Planters for Wildlife Make your autumn landscape even more alluring with simple yet stellar pots and planters.

118 Fall Birding Basics Attract more birds to your backyard this autumn.

120 Year-Round Butterflies: Autumn Learn how butterflies prepare for the cooler days ahead.

121 Glad You Asked Find expert answers to your fall wildlife garden queries.

123 Backyard Builders These woodworkers scaled down cozy cabins with feathered friends in mind.

124 Upcycled Bird Feeder Turn old odds and ends into a distinctive bird feeder.

126 Pie Tin Bird Feeder Serve up a feast anytime in this durable feeder.

127 Hummingbird Feeder for Pennies Give yourself the best view in the house with a tiny window feeder for flying jewels.

128 Autumn Garden Gallery Catch a glimpse of Mother Nature's finest fall offerings.

130 Wonders of Winter

132 Winter Backyard Checklist Keep the wildlife coming with our cold-weather checklist.

134 Winter Wonderland Follow these three simple steps to provide a warm wintertime welcome to your feathered friends.

138 The Best Plant Picks for Winter Wildlife These plants help birds stay safe and well fed through the coldest months.

144 An Enchanting Winter Garden Spread a little magic through your yard, no matter what weather Mother Nature has in store.

146 Dazzling Winter Containers Visiting birds are here to stay with these seasonal planters.

148 Winter Birding Basics When the chill rolls in, so do birds! Here's what you should know now.

150 Year-Round Butterflies: Winter Find out what your favorite butterflies are up to at the chilliest time of the year.

151 Glad You Asked Experts answer your most pressing winter questions.

153 Backyard Builders These fun projects help you include wildlife in your holiday plans.

154 Plantable Gift Tags Recycle your junk mail and encourage green thumbs.

156 A Feast for Birds Treat your feathered friends to a festive midwinter snack.

157 Feeder From a Frame Turn an old picture frame into a delightful bird feeder.

158 Winter Garden Gallery See the true essence of winter, captured in photographs.

160 Gardener's Field Guides

160 North American Birds Get to know the avian visitors to your own backyard.

180 North American Butterflies Meet the winged jewels that are most likely to stop by your garden.

190 Index

192 Zone Map What plants will thrive where you live?

welcoming WILDLIFE

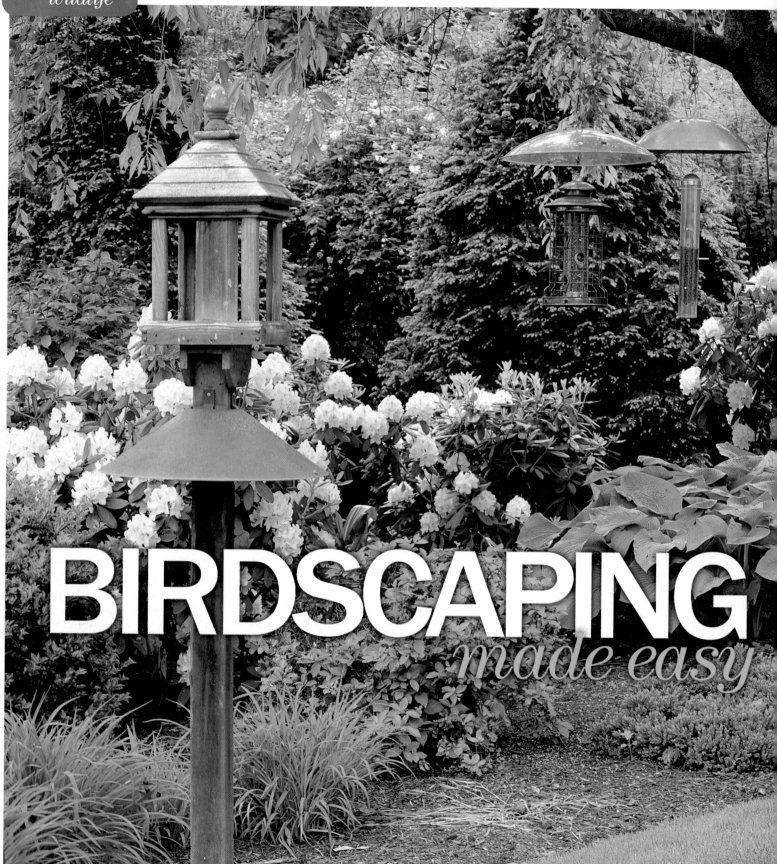

BIRDSCAPING
made easy

Make your backyard irresistible with just a few easy tricks. BY SALLY ROTH

Put up a feeder, pour in some seed and you'll attract birds.

Yes, it really is that simple. Food is the first step to winning the hearts of birds, and keeping a feeder makes you feel good, too.

But a feeder is just the beginning. To really bring in the birds—more birds, of more species—you need to make them feel at home in your yard. And the way to do that is with plants.

"Birdscaping," as some call it, is a lot simpler than it sounds. All it takes are a few lessons and some common sense from the very best gardener of all: Mother Nature!

Safety First

All birds are sitting ducks when it comes to predators. A stalking cat may rush the robin on the lawn. A hungry hawk may drop from the sky at any moment. Vulnerable nestlings, eggs or even parent birds on the nest may be the target of a prowling raccoon or slithering snake.

Only a few birds, including blackbirds and robins, spend a lot of time in the open. Most of our feathered friends, however, stay under cover as much as they can to boost their chances of survival.

Here's where nature's lessons come in handy. Just imitate natural wild areas, and you've got it made. You could just let your whole backyard go wild; birds would heartily approve. But most of us like to keep some sense of order, so try these tricks to keep both you and your birds happy:

- **PLANT SHRUBS IN GROUPS** of three or more, to build larger areas of cover.
- **SPREAD A THICK LAYER** of mulch beneath and between shrubs, and instantly, you've created an inviting foraging area for towhees, robins, native sparrows and even juncos.

MIX IT UP. A successful wildlife garden combines flowers and foliage, trees and shrubs to create an environment that offers food and shelter to a wide range of our feathered friends.

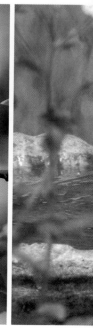

A GOOD SIGN

Keep an eye out for nesters, whether they built their own nest in a backyard tree or shrub, smack-dab in your hanging basket of petunias or in a birdhouse you made last winter. The presence of nesting birds is a sign that your birdscaping is working. You've succeeded in making the birds feel at home, and that's cause for celebration! How about planting another berry bush to mark the occasion?

NATIVE OR NOT? Birds love nearly every native berry—as long as it's an "unimproved" species. When breeders tinker with them, aiming for bigger, brighter berries, the bird appeal can get lost. The crop on new varieties of crabapples and deciduous hollies, which were once bona fide bird plants, often goes uneaten.

- **ADD A HEDGE** along a boundary or your privacy fence. Include thorny shrubs, such as barberry, roses or flowering quince, to provide tempting nesting places for brown thrashers, gray catbirds, northern cardinals and others.
- **PLANT EVERGREEN SHRUBS** and trees like holly, rhododendron and spruce to offer shelter from the weather in all seasons.
- **VARY THE HEIGHT** of your flower beds and boost their bird appeal by planting small trees— flowering crab, dogwood and redbud, for example—right in the beds.

Blooming Bird Feeders

Talk about multitasking—the plants in our yards do it all. They supply vital protective cover, shelter birds in bad weather and serve as nesting places.

And that's not all. Many plants also serve up enough natural food—seeds, fruit, berries and especially bugs—to keep our feathered friends coming back day after day.

Insects are the natural food that birds rely on year-round. A big banquet of them will draw in songbirds of all kinds, just as feeders do.

To boost your bugs—yep, more insects is a good thing, if you want birds—add spring-flowering trees to your yard. Crabapples and other fruit trees bloom at migration time. That makes them an

inviting pit stop for traveling wood warblers, vireos, gnatcatchers, tanagers, orioles and other birds that recognize the opportunity for a feast.

Caterpillars are another can't-miss menu item. They're at their peak during nesting season, just in time to stuff down a bunch of gaping beaks. No need to research good plants for caterpillars—just go native. Many native trees, shrubs and other plants serve as hosts for egg-laying butterflies or moths, as well as nurturing a plethora of other beneficial insects.

Of course, you'll want to avoid pesticides as much as possible in your bird paradise—see "Chemical-Free Control" for more info on eco-friendly garden products. Think of those pesky bugs as bird food, and be patient until the troops arrive. Wrens, chickadees and vireos help out with aphids. Cardinals and rose-breasted grosbeaks snap up potato beetles. And starlings are your best friends when it comes to those pretty but damaging Japanese beetles: They're searching for grubs when they waddle about, stabbing the ground.

Fruits and Berries

Ask any bird lover what plants are best for birds, and the answer is likely to be berry bushes.

Birds somehow know when the fruit crop is ready, and it's quite a thrill when our favorite

songbirds—bluebirds, rose-breasted grosbeaks, waxwings and more—start winging their way in from miles around.

Still, it takes only a week or so until the birds have gobbled every berry. The show is over until the next fruit or berry in your yard starts to ripen.

I wouldn't be without berry bushes or fruit trees in my yard. But I look beyond the harvest, and so do the birds. Any fruit or berry we plant is going to be home to bugs. Even if they escape our notice, birds will find them. Plus, like any plant we find a place for, berry bushes will add to the available cover, and maybe even cradle a nest come spring.

The Power of Water

A reliable source of fresh water can be more powerful than the best-stocked feeder. At migration time and during the long, hot summer, your birdbath is likely to get more traffic than your feeding station.

The vessel's style doesn't matter, as long as the basin isn't too slippery for birds to get a grip. Birds will find water, whether it's a puddle of rainwater in your wheelbarrow or a nifty waterfall you spent a weekend setting up.

The key words are reliable and fresh. Keep your birdbath clean and filled, so winged visitors know they can count on a sip and a splash at your place.

chemical-free control
Keep weeds and pests at bay without harming wildlife.

BY **MELINDA MYERS**

As wildlife gardeners, we are always trying to maintain "green" gardens that are beautiful and safe. Fortunately, there are lots of products that can help us manage unwelcome visitors.

A new group of pest management tools are plant protection products like JAZ spray (a product I endorse). Scientists isolated and replicated the chemicals some plants produce when dealing with stress and pests to create products we can use to "immunize" our plants. Several applications of these types of products help build the plants' natural defenses.

Soaps and plant oils, such as Neem, are also entering the pest-control market. Small amounts help repel, kill and control many insects and some diseases.

Iron phosphate is the active ingredient in Sluggo and other relatively new eco-friendly slug and snail controls. The iron phosphate acts as a stomach poison for the slugs but does not harm the birds, toads or pets that eat the poisoned slug.

Spinosad is another new type of pest control product. It is classed as organic, breaks down quickly and is shown to have minimal negative effect on beneficial insects.

Biologicals such as *Bacillus thuringiensis* (Bt) have been available for years, with several strains used to kill the larvae of caterpillars, gnats, mosquitoes and potato beetles. Additional types with a wider range of controls are now on the market.

Continue to invite beneficial insects into your landscape by avoiding insecticides and tolerating a bit of damage. After all, you need a food source to bring in the good guys.

go NATIVE

Attract more birds and butterflies by including native plants in your landscape. BY MELINDA MYERS

Switchgrass

Prairie Coneflower

Take a tour of your landscape. You may be surprised to learn that quite a few native plants have already found their way into your yard. Many plant breeders, designers and garden centers have included natives in their collections, making it easier for you to do the same.

Of course, whether you're buying natives or hybrids, it's important to select the right plants for your growing conditions. But with these ideas you'll be on your way to a more natural, wildlife-friendly backyard.

Start Small

The best place to begin is to look at natives in their natural habitat. That way, you can see what plants perform well, which ones look good together and which are bullies. Use cultivars of your favorite native for a tamer growth habit suited to the space.

For example, switchgrass (*Panicum*) is a beautiful, adaptive but rapidly spreading grass. It's ideal for large natural plantings or along roadways, but it will take over a typical backyard. Cultivars like Northwind, Heavy Metal (left) and Shenandoah are clumpers that do not readily reseed. Start small if you're hesitant to include this grass, or if you have limited space.

Have a shady spot? Woodland wildflowers are a good choice for heavily shaded areas. Such natives may just be the perfect solution for those sun-deprived places in your yard where other flowers won't grow.

All Natives, All the Time

Perhaps you're contemplating making the leap and filling your yard exclusively with native plants. Good for you for going full force! Consult an expert before digging in too much. Proper soil preparation and weed control are essential for establishing plants and getting them to flourish.

Buy locally grown plants and seeds whenever possible, and remember that not all seeds are created equal. Some wildflower or native grass seed packages include "fillers"—native plants that can be aggressive and undesirable in your region. Locally produced seed may cost more per pound, but it's a better value in the long run.

When converting your landscape to a natural paradise, keep neighbors in mind. An edge of mowed grass, a bit of fencing or a birdhouse can send signs of civilization to neighbors who might not share your enthusiasm for the informal look. A little compromise in the beginning may even get more neighbors to join your efforts.

As you plan, keep in mind that you may be trying to squeeze a hundred-acre plant community onto a small suburban lot. This means you'll need to help nature along to keep things in balance. And be patient. It could take a few years for your native planting to reach its full potential. But the effort will be well worth it when that peak is achieved and birds and butterflies fill your garden, enjoying their native habitat.

CONEFLOWER: CAROLYN CARNEY; SWITCHGRASS: PERENNIAL RESOURCE.COM; NATIVE PLANTS CHART: NEW DIRECTIONS

Native Plants Chart

	COMMON NAME	SCIENTIFIC NAME	HARDINESS ZONES	FLOWER COLOR	HEIGHT	BLOOM TIME	SOIL MOISTURE
DRY SOILS AND DRY CLIMATES (15"–25" ANNUAL PRECIPITATION)	Leadplant	Amorpha canescens	3-8	Purple	2' - 3'	June-July	D, M
	Butterfly weed	Asclepias tuberosa	3-10	Orange	2' - 3'	June-Aug.	D, M
	Smooth aster	Aster laevis	4-8	Blue	2' - 4'	Aug.-Oct.	D, M
	Cream false indigo	Baptisia bracteata	4-9	Cream	1' - 2'	May-June	D, M
	Purple prairie clover	Dalea purpurea	3-8	Purple	1' - 2'	July-Aug.	D, M
	Pale purple coneflower	Echinacea pallida	4-8	Purple	3' - 5'	June-July	D, M
	Prairie smoke	Geum triflorum	3-6	Pink	6"	May-June	D, M
	Dotted blazing star	Liatris punctata	3-9	Purple/Pink	1' - 2'	Aug.-Oct.	D, M
	Wild lupine	Lupinus perennis	3-8	Blue	1' - 2'	May-June	D
	Large-flowered beardtongue	Penstemon grandiflorus	3-7	Lavender	2' - 4'	May-June	D
	Showy goldenrod	Solidago speciosa	3-8	Yellow	1' - 3'	Aug.-Sept.	D, M
	Bird's-foot violet	Viola pedata	3-9	Blue	6"	Apr.-June	D
MEDIUM SOILS IN AVERAGE RAINFALL CLIMATES (25"–45" ANNUAL PRECIPITATION)	Nodding pink onion	Allium cernuum	3-8	White/Pink	1' - 2'	July-Aug.	M, Mo
	New England aster	Aster novae-angliae	3-7	Blue/Purple	3' - 6'	Aug.-Sept.	M, Mo
	Blue false indigo	Baptisia australis	3-10	Blue	3' - 5'	June-July	M, Mo
	White false indigo	Baptisia lactea	4-9	White	3' - 5'	June-July	M, Mo
	Shooting star	Dodecatheon meadia	4-8	White/Pink	1' - 2'	May-June	M, Mo
	Purple coneflower	Echinacea purpurea	4-8	Purple	3' - 4'	July-Sept.	M, Mo
	Rattlesnake master	Eryngium yuccifolium	4-9	White	3' - 5'	June-Aug.	M
	Prairie blazing star	Liatris pycnostachya	3-9	Purple/Pink	3' - 5'	July-Aug.	M, Mo
	Wild quinine	Parthenium integrifolium	4-8	White	3' - 5'	June-Sept.	M, Mo
	Yellow coneflower	Ratibida pinnata	3-9	Yellow	3' - 6'	July-Sept.	M, Mo
	Royal catchfly	Silene regia	4-9	Red	2' - 4'	July-Aug.	M
	Stiff goldenrod	Solidago rigida	3-9	Yellow	3' - 5'	Aug.-Sept.	M, Mo
MOIST SOILS AND MOIST CLIMATES (45"–60" ANNUAL PRECIPITATION)	Wild hyacinth	Camassia scilloides	4-8	White	1' - 2'	May-June	M, Mo
	Tall Joe Pye weed	Eupatorium fistulosum	4-9	Purple/Pink	5' - 8'	Aug.-Sept.	Mo, W
	Queen of the prairie	Filipendula rubra	3-6	Pink	4' - 5'	June-July	M, Mo
	Bottle gentian	Gentiana andrewsii	3-6	Blue	1' - 2'	Aug.-Oct.	Mo, W
	Rose mallow	Hibiscus palustris	4-9	Pink	3' - 6'	July-Sept.	Mo, W
	Dense blazing star	Liatris spicata	4-10	Purple/Pink	3' - 6'	Aug.-Sept.	Mo, W
	Cardinal flower	Lobelia cardinalis	3-9	Red	2' - 5'	July-Sept.	Mo, W
	Marsh phlox	Phlox glaberrima	4-8	Red/ Purple	2' - 4'	June-July	M, Mo
	Sweet black-eyed Susan	Rudbeckia subtomentosa	3-9	Yellow	4' - 6'	Aug.-Oct.	M, Mo
	Ohio goldenrod	Solidago ohioensis	4-5	Yellow	3' - 4'	Aug.-Sept.	M, Mo
	Tall ironweed	Vernonia altissima	4-9	Red/Pink	5' - 8'	Aug.-Sept.	Mo, W
	Culver's root	Veronicastrum virginicum	3-8	White	3' - 6'	July-Aug.	M, Mo

SOIL MOISTURE KEY
D = Dry (Well-drained sandy and rocky soils), M = Medium (Normal garden soils such as loam, sandy loam and clay loam), Mo = Moist (Soils that stay moist below the surface, but are not boggy; may dry out in late summer), W = Wet (Soils that are continually moist through the growing season, subject to short periods of spring flooding)

wildlife landscaper Q&A

What's a good **rule of thumb when it comes to planting** gardens for birds and butterflies?

DR: Make sure it is more than just a stopover for a quick meal. Use native plants that offer food, shelter and nesting opportunities.

DOP: Include native diversity, and skip the horticultural varieties. Those bred for extended bloom or color have often lost their nectar.

RS: As in all good design, the garden needs to be interesting year-round—not only for humans, but for wildlife.

PP: It's best not to be too tidy. A garden for birds and butterflies is a relaxed garden, with frostbitten plants like coneflower and ornamental grasses left standing for seed and shelter. Instead of a fall clean-up, do a late winter one in preparation for spring.

What do you try to include in every **habitat design**?

DR: I like to include some native flowering ground covers, such as foamflower and wild geranium. And I always incorporate a quiet, secluded seating area so people can enjoy the garden and its wildlife.

PP: I also plant plenty of midlevel plants— between the trees and ground covers—to offer shelter.

RS: I encourage clients to provide more than one water source. Small, shallow dishes or birdbaths offer easy access for little birds. Larger, deeper birdbaths are perfect for bigger birds and those that bathe in groups.

What are your **tricks for small-space** wildlife gardeners?

PP: Make the most of every inch: Choose plants that produce flowers or berries and look good all year. A small flowering tree gives some shade to the gardener and cover for birds, and structural evergreen shrubs carry the space through the year. You can tuck flowers around them.

RS: Focus on vertical plants. One of my favorite techniques is to plant a large climbing rose along a fence to provide a safe environment for many birds.

DR: Lots of hummingbird- and butterfly-attracting vines can be grown on trellises placed in containers. Annual vines such as scarlet runner beans offer food for the birds and butterflies and for you and your family.

DOP: One thing we do at EnergyScapes that is more unusual is convert driveways into drivable gardens to expand habitat.

How about **gardens in urban areas**?

RS: In an urban setting, the distance between open spaces can make it difficult for birds or insects to find food or a place to rest. Planted balconies and courtyards act as rest stops, also known as an urban wildlife corridor.

PP: Use planters, or even plant a green roof with low-growing, drought-tolerant flowering plants and grasses. And a small fountain will attract birds to your space. For safety's sake, know the weight limits before adding heavy potted plants or water features.

DOP: A big question is how to blend with the neighbors. Screen buffers of gray dogwood and lower shrubs at the edges are awesome.

Believe it or not, some people are lucky enough to call gardening for birds and butterflies their life's work. Here, four landscape designers offer their secrets to hosting your favorite fliers.

Which plants keep **unwanted wildlife** at bay?

DOP: Try thorny native plants, such as locust, hawthorn and greenbrier.

PP: Plants with strongly scented leaves will help stop deer from browsing your garden: herbs like rosemary and oregano, lantana, Powis Castle artemisia, autumn sage and Mexican mint marigold.

DR: I like to interplant aromatic plants with others that deer might favor.

To entice songbirds, Rebecca plants large shrubs such as firethorn. **It's lovely in winter** and provides a natural source for food and shelter.

the panelists

These designers specialize in gardens for birds and butterflies. Read gardening tales and landscape ideas on their blogs.

Douglas Owens-Pike
EnergyScapes
St. Paul, MN
energyscapes.com/blog

Pam Penick
Penick Landscape
Design ~ Austin, TX
penick.net/digging

Deborah Roberts
Roberts & Roberts
Landscape and Garden
Design ~ Stamford, CT
gardenofpossibilities.com

Rebecca Sweet
Harmony in the Garden
Los Altos, CA
gossipinthegarden.com

pacific
PARADISE

CRAZY FOR CONTAINERS.
To add color and texture
to his yard, Richard placed
containers like these in
walkways and on patios.

In just a few short years, one gardener transformed a hillside retreat into a bird and butterfly haven.

BY ANN WILSON

When an experienced gardener wields his green thumb in Washington state's temperate climes, the result is amazingly gorgeous views. Dr. Richard Driscoll is such a gardener. In just a few years he's converted a lackluster 3-acre site into a lush landscape that not only provides him with a creative respite from a hectic career, but is also home to bevies of birds and butterflies.

Richard and his wife, Pam, bought the Vashon Island home as a weekend retreat in 2005 and immediately saw potential in the weedy pasture that sloped steeply away from the hilltop house.

"We had been in a home with a shady yard for 16 years," Richard recalls, "and we were looking for a place with lots of sun for growing perennials. This property offered great views of the harbor and gave me a blank slate for planting."

A Frenzy of Flowers

Before Richard could dig in, excavators terraced the hillsides and contractors installed rocky walls and stone stairways to connect upper terraces to those below.

"We brought in yards and yards of topsoil," Richard says. "Then, working in five phases, I did one garden a year, planting each and every plant myself. I started the gardens with structural plants like flowering shrubs and small trees, and then added perennials.

"I've been gardening for 35 years and have always loved flowers, but now I'm getting into foliage and textures," adds Richard. "I love to use every flower color to mix things up."

He handily combines his favorite plants— hydrangeas, roses, lilacs, flame-leafed coral bells and bright-red dianthus—with sprawling sedums and blue-flowering lithodora in borders that spill over into seating areas and pathways. Vast plantings of purple-leafed coral bells, ornamental grasses and fragrant lavenders ramble across a hillside. Nectar-rich hummingbird magnets, including cape fuchsia, azalea, wisteria, trumpet

TERRY DONNELLY

vine, agastache, lupine and foxglove, pop up across the landscape.

"We have a ton of hummingbirds in our garden," says Richard. "They really like the tubular yellow, red and orange flowers. There seem to be flowers for them during most of the season."

A Fully Stocked Garden

In addition to his perennial borders, Richard tends a vegetable garden that spans 12 raised planting beds and dozens of raspberry and blueberry bushes, a fruit orchard and 55 containers that he plants with spring-blooming bulbs, then replants in May with vibrant annuals.

"There's a lot of planting going on at our house," Richard explains with a wide grin. "The pots are really important to the overall design. I think of containers as artwork that supply long-term interest."

He positions the statuesque containers to define entry points to paths and stairways and to enhance courtyards and borders. Along with the weathered structures and whimsical garden ornaments, they ensure that there's something worth seeing at every turn. As he works on new gardens, Richard also tweaks those he planted in the past—his landscape is always evolving, so garden views shift from year to year.

"I do a lot of re-creating, and I don't necessarily follow all the rules," he notes. "You do the best you can with the time you have, which means that I divide and move plants all year long. And I plant things close together because I don't like to see bare spots."

Densely packed gardens keep Pam well stocked with fresh-picked bouquets and a bounty of homegrown produce for meals. Outdoor rooms overlooking watery vistas invite the couple and their guests to linger.

"Pam and I relax on the patios, and occasionally entertain in the garden," says Richard. "I spend most of my weekends cultivating, weeding and planting. Gardening is the only thing I do that is really creative. I love to give areas a fun look."

TOP LEFT, FAR RIGHT: MARK LUTZ/ALLEN IN; BOTTOM LEFT, NEAR RIGHT: JERRY DONNELLY

BACK TO BASICS. Over the years, Richard has picked up this wise gardening advice: Use the best soil. He plants in a 50-50 mix of compost and soil for easy root growth and drainage. Next, fertilize strategically. Richard fertilizes his gardens yearly and adds it to new planting holes. Last, compost religiously. Ensure soil has plenty of nutrients by generously spreading compost each spring.

planters for wildlife

Butterflies and hummingbirds love containers filled with their favorite plants. Watch them enjoy your yard with these three container tips:

1. Offer nectar at different levels. Create a multilayered effect with different-size plants.

2. A flower's color, shape and scent will attract, but the biggest draw is the nectar.

3. Include nectar-rich, tubular flowers as well as plants with daisylike blooms. Go a step further and add a few butterfly host plants.

CONTAINER FAVORITES

Aster

Calibrachoa

Floss flower

Fuchsia

Hibiscus

Lantana

Pentas

Verbena

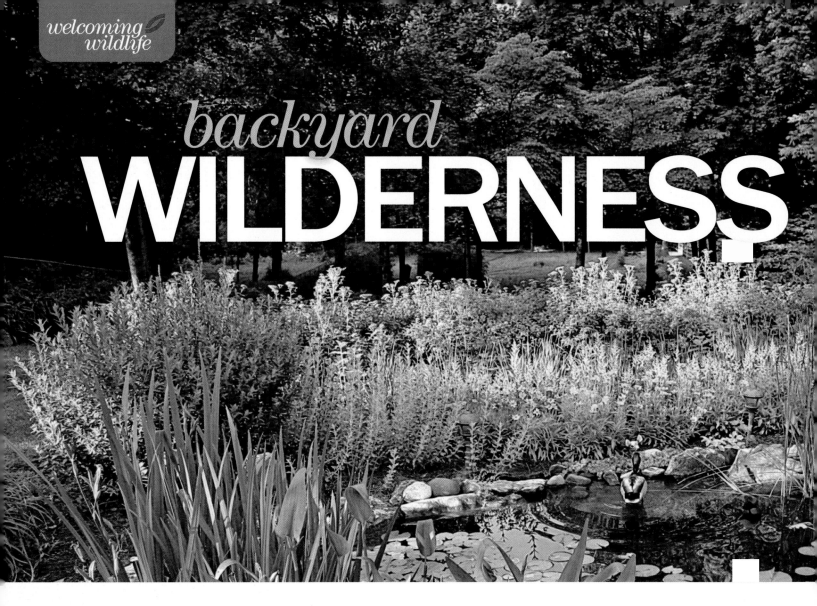

backyard WILDERNESS

From a large pond to native plants, this Kentucky reader's garden is an oasis for wildlife. STORY AND PHOTOS BY **MIKE MATTHEWS**

TAKE A SEAT. It's not hard to find a spot to relax in Mike's backyard. There's plenty to look at, such as the pond, stream and flowers like wild geranium (top right). A large variety of birds visit the backyard, too, including these pileated woodpeckers (lower right).

Thirty years ago, I saw a magazine article that changed the way I garden. *National Wildlife* ran a story about how to take an average-size suburban yard and turn it into a small wilderness by planting trees, shrubs and other greenery to attract wildlife.

That article planted a seed in me as a young man, and I knew it would grow.

A few years later, I found a house in the suburbs of Louisville, Kentucky, on a little over an acre of semiwooded land, with a creek running through it. When the agent first showed me the property, I spotted a great horned owl and its three babies at the bottom of a hill. I knew then and there that this was my piece of heaven on earth.

Going Native

For more than 20 years, I've been working hard to create the best wildlife habitat I can. Along the way, I've replaced the non-native and invasive plants with such bird favorites as winterberries, serviceberries and more. Our reward is regular sightings of more than 60 species of birds.

One of my best sources for natives has been building sites. I rescue plants from developers just before they start to clear the land. You have to get permission, but I've never had a problem with this. This free method of acquiring plants has led to some great finds, like redbuds, native dogwoods and a variety of native flowers. If you're looking for

natives, find out if your state department of fish and wildlife has a native-plant or backyard-certification program.

Seasons of Bloom

Our yard comes alive with each new season. In spring, you'll see trillium, mayflowers and daffodils. Grosbeaks stop to eat sunflower seeds, and mallards raise their young by our pond.

As we move into summer, the purple coneflowers, butterfly weed and trumpet vine bloom, and the butterflies and hummingbirds are everywhere. Some of my favorite summer visitors are the pileated woodpeckers.

As fall approaches, we get a sudden burst of color thanks to ironweed and asters. Butterflies like these late-season blooms, and cedar waxwings show up to eat berries.

worthy of an award

In 2008, the Kentucky Department of Fish and Wildlife even named our place the best backyard habitat in the state, which was a real honor. More than anything, we hope our efforts encourage others.

field of DREAMS

This Detroit transplant learned to love the Kansas soil.

STORY AND PHOTOS BY **LENORA LARSEN**

"Plant it and they will come" is the butterfly gardener's mantra. My field of dreams began in 1981, when a job transfer moved me from downtown Detroit to rural Kansas. Twenty years of gardening in Michigan had not prepared me for conditions in Kansas, where my Zone 6 location features heavy clay soil, floods, tornadoes, lengthy droughts, incessant winds, oppressive summers and winter temperatures that can fluctuate between zero and 60 degrees in 24 hours.

But I also had some advantages, including a natural gas well for free energy and a lake for free water. I also discovered an unlimited supply of limestone slabs underneath my clay soil. This would eventually provide great building material for walls, paths and raised beds.

A 100-year-old farmhouse had recently been moved to the property, but the yard was a clean slate. In the end, my biggest advantage was my mother, a landscape designer. After several days of studying and measuring, she drew up the master plan that still guides me decades later.

A Traditional Approach

We decided that the English landscape style, with its great sweeps of beds, would fit the site's scale. Yellow, purple and silver foliage would provide drama and continuity with five stalwarts: goldmound spirea, purple smoke tree, catmint, Powis Castle artemisia and purple castor beans.

I work full time and am the sole caretaker of a 4-acre garden that will continue to expand. How do I manage? Native shrubs and vines, vigorous perennials and self-sowing annuals minimize maintenance. A thick layer of mulch controls weeds and improves the soil. With no pesticides, birds play a big role by gobbling bugs and spreading seeds.

As I expanded the gardens, my first epiphany was the hopelessness of improving the soil. No plant should be forced to live in a bed of Kansas clay and limestone. So the raised beds were dug

out and refilled with a good planting mix consisting of well-composted manure.

The second epiphany was that those stinky dill worms I'd been killing were butterfly caterpillars. Will I ever recover from the grief and guilt of hurting baby butterflies?

A New Inspiration

These graceful winged creatures are my priority. I already had many native wildflowers, but successful butterfly gardening means supplying the native foliage that is a caterpillar's diet. Unlike adults that sip nectar from a variety of flowers, butterfly caterpillars are persnickety.

These days, joy has replaced my initial frustration. My native plants are unfazed by floods, droughts and 50-mile-an-hour summer breezes. The process of researching, finding, planting and eventually welcoming a new species of butterfly is incredibly satisfying.

Each summer, the tropical brilliance of my Kansas garden rivals any commercial butterfly house. When you plant for caterpillars, butterflies fulfill the promise of the field of dreams.

BUTTERFLIES FIRST. Lenora enjoys welcoming butterflies, such as the female spicebush swallowtail (top left), to her yard. To entice monarchs, she grows milkweed (lower right).

monarch watch

To attract monarch butterflies to my landscape, I planted milkweed. The University of Kansas' Monarch Watch program—which aims to reverse habitat loss and support migration across the U.S. and Canada—certified my yard as Monarch Waystation #875.

Find out more about ways you can become involved at *monarchwatch.org.*

wake up to SPRING

wake up to spring

spring BACKYARD *checklist*

Get an early start with these seasonal to-do's.

Kick Off the Gardening Season

☐ **PRUNE** summer-flowering shrubs, including blue spirea, summersweet and rose of Sharon, to encourage bushy growth and masses of nectar-laden blooms.

☐ **INSPECT** the trees and shrubs in your yard for overwintering pests. Removing egg masses of eastern tent caterpillars, gypsy moths and other voracious insects can greatly reduce plant damage without the use of chemicals—a major goal for any wildlife gardener.

☐ **REMOVE** and compost plant debris that stayed in the garden over winter. The birds have likely picked the seed heads clean.

☐ **PREPARE** the soil and plant annuals, perennials, trees and shrubs that will attract wildlife. Include those that offer food as well as shelter.

☐ **SCOUR** garden centers for plants birds and butterflies love. Refer to our seasonal plant profiles and check plant tags for info on varieties that attract our favorite fliers.

Male bluebirds **courageously guard the box** during nest construction.

BUILDING BASICS. Bluebird nests are made of dried grasses, pine needles, weed stems and fine twigs, and are lined with finer grasses, hairs and feathers. The female does most of the work.

Spring is finally here, and it's time to start anew. From hanging birdhouses to preparing your flower beds and vegetable garden for a fresh growing season, there's a lot to do in the backyard. Tackle these important tasks now, so you can get outside and enjoy all that nature has to offer when the weather turns warm!

Create a Safe Haven

☐ **OFFER** birds nesting materials, such as string and yarn. Put them outdoors in a mesh bag or an empty suet cage, and birds will quickly notice.

☐ **BLUEBIRDS** (left) are among the earliest nesters. They often use man-made housing and like it to face open fields, so make sure yours is! Mount the proper house on a pole that's 5 to 10 feet high, and watch for starlings and house sparrows that are trying to move in.

☐ **RE-HANG** your birdhouses. If you'd like to have more and are feeling the creative itch, why not build one or two? Decide which birds you'd like to attract and see our building guidelines at *birdsandblooms.com*.

☐ **CLEAN** out the birdhouses you left standing throughout the winter to get rid of any potentially harmful parasites or bacteria. While you're at it, give your birdbath and feeders a good scouring, too.

Attract the Birds You Want

☐ **STARLINGS** can dominate feeders, so break their habit by switching to safflower seed. Grackles, starlings and squirrels dislike this food, while cardinals, titmice, house finches and chickadees love it.

☐ **FILL** your bird feeders daily. Natural food is in short supply in early spring, but migration is in full swing.

☐ **PROVIDE** oranges to lure orioles (right), grosbeaks, tanagers and house finches to your backyard. And late spring is a good time to make a batch of sugar water for returning hummers.

☐ **DESPITE** warming temperatures, keep replenishing your suet block. Even true beef suet won't get soft until it reaches about 80 degrees.

Host Butterflies

☐ **SPRING** is prime time for local garden clubs and nature groups to promote butterflies. Look for upcoming events in your area.

☐ **WATCH** for the eggs and emergence of spring azure butterflies around flowering dogwood trees, their host plant.

☐ **CHECK** flowers for nectaring butterflies that have recently emerged from wintering chrysalises.

☐ **NOW** is the ideal time to purchase and plant butterfly host trees, especially in Southern regions, where soil conditions are stable.

☐ **PLANT** dill (below), parsley and carrots for black swallowtails.

BLUEBIRD: STEVE AND DAVE MASLOWSKI; ORIOLE: ROLF NUSSBAUMER / NATUREPL.COM; DILL: THE COOK'S GARDEN

BUTTERFLY
gardening on a budget

Attract flying flowers to your yard without spending a lot of money on plants. BY TOM ALLEN

The snow has melted, trees and flowers are in bloom and garden centers are loaded with plants. It's the perfect time of year to start a butterfly garden in your backyard. You don't have to break the bank to buy plants, though. There are many readily available budget-friendly options that will attract your favorite fliers.

Magical Milkweed

Monarchs are one of the most popular butterflies. Luckily, it doesn't take much to lure these beauties into your garden. Just plant milkweed—this is the monarch's host plant, and you can easily find different low-cost types at most local nurseries. Keep in mind that there are several milkweed species, and some will be more suited to your area than others. But overall, milkweed serves as an excellent nectar source for monarchs and many other butterflies as well.

Another excellent source for many butterfly species is butterfly bush. These plants are budget-friendly, and do well in most climates. When picking varieties, the best colors for butterflies are deep purple and lavender. Beware, however, that they are considered invasive in some regions.

Other good nectar plants include phlox, an excellent border plant, and lilacs for spring blooms. Good summer options include mint, blazing stars, thistle and purple coneflower. If you want blooms that will continue through fall, consider asters, zinnias and yarrow.

If you're looking to get lots of flowers for not a lot of money, then annuals like violas, pansies and nasturtiums are perfect for your garden. They easily grow from seed or are inexpensive choices at garden centers or from seed catalogs. Plus, they attract a wide range of butterflies.

Violets are the host plant for most fritillaries. Pansies (and also Johnny-jump-ups) are good for attracting variegated fritillaries.

Make a Long-Term Impact

Small trees and shrubs are essential for any butterfly garden. In my own flower beds in Florida, one of my favorite shrubs is leadwort or blue plumbago. It has beautiful blue flowers on which the cassius blue caterpillar feeds. I also have the white-flowered native species of this, but I've noticed the butterflies prefer the blue blossoms to the white ones.

Bahama cassia and privet cassia shrubs offer nice clusters of yellow flowers and attract the cloudless sulphur, a species that will invade northern states in favorable years.

One of my favorite butterflies is the orange-barred sulphur, which comes to my dwarf species of tree senna. I also love swallowtails, and for these beauties, I have three different pipevine species along my fence to attract the polydamus or gold-rim varieties.

If you are able, plant your butterfly garden near a wooded area. Many butterflies like to stay close to the cover of trees, so this would allow you to attract even more species.

You don't always need blooms to attract butterflies. Some common lawn grasses and even weeds are important butterfly host plants.

Take clovers for example. They are host plants for the eastern tailed-blue, various sulphurs and cloudywing skippers. Lawn grasses are host plants to various skippers. Wood nymphs will also use the grasses if you let them grow tall in small patches at the edges of your yard.

There is no secret formula for bringing in butterflies. If you're willing to spend a little extra time in the garden experimenting with a variety of plants, you're likely to be successful. Keep in mind, some of your most desired butterflies may not appear in the first year.

But you should never have to spend a fortune. Hopefully, this is just the start of hosting butterflies in your backyard.

NECTAR KNOWLEDGE. The amount of nectar a bloom produces can vary within a species. A good rule of thumb is to go with species plants whenever possible, rather than cultivars.

out on a LIMB

Hummingbird nests are individual pieces of art. BY GEORGE HARRISON

LITTLE WONDERS. The rufous (above) is the most northern of hummingbirds, migrating as far as Alaska. The female black-chinned hummer (right) is in charge of feeding her young, who take off after just 3 weeks.

Like a crown jewel, the nest of a hummingbird is one of the great wonders in all of nature. They are so tiny, yet so perfect.

Few of us have ever seen a hummingbird nest. This is because they are nearly impossible to find. From the ground, they look like another bump on a branch. From above, an umbrella of leaves conceals them. And from the side, they look like a tiny knot, quilted with lichens, plant down and fibers.

Though each of the 17 hummingbird species that breed in North America builds slightly different nests in various habitats, they have many things in common. For example, all females build their nests 10 to 90 feet high in trees or shrubs.

All hummingbirds use spider silk as threads to bind their nests together and anchor them to the foundation. In addition, all build velvety, compact cups with spongy floors and elastic sides that stretch as the young grow.

Most hummingbirds lay two white eggs about the size of navy beans. The females continue to add material to their nests while they incubate the eggs for 15 to 18 days. The young leave the nests 18 to 28 days after hatching.

While these are the basics for hummingbird nests, it is interesting to see what makes each of these species unique. My father, Hal Harrison, studied bird nests for decades, and these are some of his observations. From the Allen's to the rufous, it's easy to see why these nesting creatures captivate so many people.

ALLEN'S: A birder once found an Allen's nest decorated with green paint chips peeled from a nearby picnic table.

ANNA'S: The female builds a mere platform as early as December to lay her eggs. Then she builds up the nest while incubating.

BLACK-CHINNED: The rim of the deep cup may be curved inward.

BLUE-THROATED: This hummingbird often builds its nest on electric wire inside or outside of cabins.

BROAD-BILLED: It is known to build loosely constructed nests on clotheslines.

BROAD-TAILED: This hummingbird often returns to same nesting site year after year.

CALLIOPE: This species will build a series of two, three or even four nests on top of one another, often attached to a conifer cone.

COSTA'S: These females will colonize at favorable locations with as many as six nests in a 100-foot radius. The birds are very tame at nesting sites.

MAGNIFICENT: This species builds the largest and highest of all North American hummingbird nests.

RUBY-THROATED: The female uses spider silk to attach her nest to a small twig or branch that slants downward. She covers the outside with greenish-gray lichens. Then she may lay eggs in a second nest while still feeding the young in the first.

RUFOUS: This western species is very pugnacious around its nest, often driving away much larger birds.

growing a nest
Help hummers along by planting a ready-made supply of nesting materials. BY KRIS WETHERBEE

A hummingbird's nest is composed of a variety of materials, and plants play a big role. Soft plant fibers and bits of leaves make the flexible shape that expands as the nestlings grow. Fluffy plant down and animal hair line the inside. And bits of lichen and moss cleverly camouflage the outside.

Enhance your own hummingbird habitat by growing a diversity of leafy trees and large shrubs that provide shelter at varying heights. And get more bang for your buck by planting catkin-bearing plants, which provide soft plant fibers for nesting material. Some examples include willows, witch hazel, alder, American elm, cottonwood, ironwood, poplar, birch, beech, mulberry and maple.

Grow perennials, annuals and vines with fuzzy foliage or seeds so hummers can harvest the downy fibers. The seed heads on clematis and honeysuckle transform into fuzzy balls, which hummingbirds also use.

Pasque flower and blanket flower offer similar soft fibers. Pasque flowers have soft foliage with silken hairs and mid-spring flowers followed by fuzzy seedpods. After blooming, blanket flowers form similar pods.

Lamb's ear has dense, ground-hugging rosettes of thick, woolly leaves. The silken plumes of ornamental grasses provide yet another source of nesting materials. And all milkweeds offer inflated seedpods with silky seeds.

So the next time you add to your garden, include a few nest-friendly selections to create a more hospitable habitat for hummers.

30 *plants for a stellar* SPRING GARDEN

Transform your yard with fliers in mind.

American Goldfinch in Redbud

THIS PAGE: DAVID KAY / SHUTTERSTOCK.COM: ALLIUM: RDA-GID; BLEEDING HEART: TLARA / IVANURSE7.COM; COLUMBINE: SUSAN EKSTROM; BUGLEWEED; PHLOX: PERENNIALRESOURCE.COM: FORGET-ME-NOT: MOLLY MCCUI FY

As the new growing season picks up steam, we welcome many types of flora and fauna back to our gardens. Make your yard a haven for birds and butterflies with this wide array of landscape picks.

annuals, biennials & perennials

Allium

Allium spp. • Zones 2 to 10
Looking to add a colorful bounce to your garden? There's no better bloomer than allium! This pretty perennial is a winning selection, available in shades of purple, pink, white and yellow. Not only can you find an allium to suit nearly any spot, this enchanting plant is easy to grow, and different species bloom from midspring until fall.

Bleeding Heart

Dicentra spectabilis • Zones 3 to 9
Give life to a shady spot by planting a few of these delicate perennials. Long-lasting blooms open in midspring, covering this graceful plant with gorgeous floral pendants in shades of rose pink and creamy white. Watch for a hummingbird or two hovering nearby.

Columbine

Aquilegia spp. • Zones 3 to 9
Blooming exuberantly from spring to early summer, columbine's distinctive flowers come in a wide spectrum of solids and bicolors, boasting single or double sets of petals. Plants range from 8 inches to 3 feet high. Watch for all sorts of pollinators, plus the aptly named columbine duskywing butterfly, which uses this as a host plant.

Common Bugleweed

Ajuga reptans • Zones 3 to 9
This evergreen perennial makes an excellent ground cover with its masses of bronze, green or variegated foliage. Columns of blue or pink flowers appear in spring and early summer, inviting butterflies and newly arrived hummingbirds to sip its nectar. Deer-resistant bugleweed is an aggressive grower and may invade lawns, so plant yours within a barrier. On the upside, you won't have to wait long for it to fill in after planting!

Creeping Phlox

Phlox subulata • Zones 3 to 8
Topping off at just 6 inches, creeping phlox is a smaller, mat-forming relative of the familiar fragrant perennial. When it blooms in spring, it forms a carpet of pretty little blossoms that entice passing butterflies. When nestled into a protective layer of mulch, creeping phlox doesn't require much watering.

Forget-Me-Not

Myosotis sylvatica • Zones 5 to 9
Early-season butterflies certainly remember to visit these dainty blooms, which range from the classic blue to white and pink. Though forget-me-not is considered a biennial, it produces a lot of seeds, making it a smart self-sowing ground cover.

Allium

Common Bugleweed

Bleeding Heart

Creeping Phlox

Columbine

Forget-Me-Not

Foxglove

Pinkroot

Foxglove

Digitalis spp. • Zones 3 to 10

With 18-inch to 6-foot spires covered with bright, bell-shaped blooms, this showy plant can't be missed. Self-seeding foxglove is a biennial or short-lived perennial, so leave the spent flowers in place and you'll be treated to a new crop of blooms each spring.

Lungwort

Pulmonaria spp. • Zones 2 to 8

A popular early nectar source for hummingbirds, lungwort's blue, purple, pink or white blooms and dappled leaves lend interest to shady backyards. The foliage often remains green clear into winter, making this plant an all-season asset. Most cultivars are about 12 inches tall and thrive in moist, well-draining soil.

Lupine

Lupinus spp. • Zones 3 to 7

Give your backyard a bit of rustic charm by planting a stand of lupines. With colors and sizes that suit any garden, varieties range from native species to new hybrids. Hummingbirds, butterflies (especially blues) and songbirds all seek out this late-spring bloomer, which prefers sun or partial shade.

Pansy

Viola x *wittrockiana*
grown as an annual

This colorful flower is best known for the whiskered "faces" that mark many of the blooms. The majority of pansies are annuals, though some live longer. Most perform best in cooler weather, so in warm climates they're valued for bringing much-needed color to dull winter landscapes.

Pinkroot

Spigelia marilandica • Zones 5 to 9

Hummers will be especially grateful that you added pinkroot to your garden. A rugged and handsome wildflower of modest size—from 1 to 2 feet tall and wide—it blooms from late spring to early summer. The spiky tube-shaped flowers are bright pink and yellow.

Rock Cress

Arabis caucasica • Zones 4 to 8

Add some springtime fragrance to your garden with this delicate bloomer. Rock cress prefers dry soil and full sun. Give this short-and-sweet ground cover a haircut after it's finished blooming to help it fill out and look tidier for the rest of the growing season.

Viola

Viola cornuta • grown as an annual

Also known as the horned violet, the faintly scented, low-maintenance viola tolerates sun and partial shade. It blooms most profusely in cool weather, when it's an ideal nectar source for cabbage whites, sulphurs, blues and others. Increase insect traffic to your garden by planting these low growers at the base of taller nectar sources.

Lungwort

Lupine

Rock Cress

Viola

Pansy

A springtime must-have, **pansies' colors run the gamut**, from multihued series such as Bingo and Atlas to monochromatic varieties ranging from white to purple to apricot.

Flowering Dogwood

Common Alder

Common Chokecherry

Fothergilla

shrubs & trees

Common Alder
Alnus glutinosa • Zones 3 to 7
If your yard is plagued by wet or just plain poor soil, consider planting common alder. Migratory birds eat the bugs on the late-winter and early-spring catkins, and winter birds eat the seeds in the cones. Eventually reaching 80 feet high and 30 feet wide, the common alder also offers plenty of shelter. Before planting, ensure that it isn't invasive in your area.

Common Chokecherry
Prunus virginiana • Zones 2 to 7
An ideal addition to a protective thicket for both birds and butterflies, chokecherry grows 20 to 30 feet high and wide. It produces clusters of pink or white flowers in spring and red berries that deepen to purple by late summer.

Flowering Dogwood
Cornus florida • Zones 5 to 8
Thanks to flowering dogwood's pink and white bracts surrounding small green flowers, butterflies and other pollinators pay frequent visits in spring. Many birds nest among the branches, and later in the growing season enjoy the bright-red berries. This lovely ornamental reaches 20 to 30 feet tall and grows best in partial to full sun.

Fothergilla
Fothergilla spp. • Zones 4 to 8
With bluish foliage that turns gold, orange and purple in fall, this shrub is a garden standout long after its fluffy spring flowers—attractive to warblers and vireos that eat resident insects—fade. Larger varieties of fothergilla reach 8 feet tall, while dwarf cultivars are less than half that size. Plant it in a sunny spot with acidic soil.

Lilac

New Jersey Tea

Pussy Willow

Mockorange

Pinkshell Azalea

Redbud

Lilac

Syringa spp. • Zones 3 to 8
Among spring's most anticipated sights and scents, the lilac attracts butterflies and hummingbirds and serves as a nesting site for songbirds. A deciduous shrub growing up to about 20 feet tall and wide, this sun lover is at its best in small groups or as a specimen plant.

Mockorange

Philadelphus spp. • Zones 3 to 11
Butterflies love this shrub's scented white spring flowers, and so will you. Varieties range in size from just 18 inches to more than 10 feet tall. Most types of mockorange prefer full sun and thrive in well-draining soil.

New Jersey Tea

Ceanothus americanus • Zones 4 to 8
A low-growing shrub 3 feet high and 5 feet wide, New Jersey tea supplies ample shelter and nectar for visiting fliers. It's also a host to some azure and duskywing butterflies. Sweet-smelling 2-inch panicles of small white flowers begin blooming in late spring.

Pinkshell Azalea

Rhododendron vaseyi • Zones 5 to 8
Brighten a partly shady woodland garden with the sweet blossoms of pinkshell azalea. This spring- and summer-blooming shrub attracts nectar-seeking fliers. Plant in a spot with plenty of room, since it can reach up to 15 feet tall. Despite the name, some varieties also bloom in white.

Pussy Willow

Salix discolor • Zones 4 to 8
In midspring, velvety silver-gray catkins emerge from the bare stems of this small upright tree. Migrating birds stop by to eat little insects on the branches, which play host to a number of butterflies once the blue-green leaves appear. Some backyard birds, like cardinals and finches, eat the flower buds as well. Plant pussy willow in moist, well-draining soil in a sunny place where it has room to expand.

Redbud

Cercis spp. • Zones 4 to 10
An early-spring showstopper, this tree bursts with a profusion of purple, red, pink or white blossoms before the leaves emerge. Redbud's blooms attract hummers, butterflies (especially hairstreaks) and other pollinators. The seeds appeal to chickadees, goldfinches and others, and nuthatches and woodpeckers eat the insects on the bark. Henry's elfin caterpillars use redbuds as a host. Plant yours where there's plenty of space, as they're often wider than they are tall.

Wisteria

Wisteria floribunda • Zones 5 to 9
There's nothing quite like a blooming garland of wisteria to add romance to a spring backyard—especially when the butterflies (including skippers, sulfurs and blues) and hummingbirds arrive. Provide ample support for the vine's heavy, woody limbs, which can extend to more than 30 feet, and prune wisteria each year after it flowers.

Wisteria

Red Buckeye

Aesculus pavia • Zones 5 to 9
In late spring, the red buckeye unfurls 6-inch-long upright panicles of tubular red flowers. It grows to just 15 feet tall and 10 feet wide, so one of these would look right at home in most backyards. Moist, well-draining soil and partial shade are the ideal growing conditions for this compact tree.

Sassafras

Sassafras albidum • Zones 4 to 7
Your yard will be a hit with fliers when you plant a sassafras tree. It's a host for some swallowtails, and more than a dozen species of birds (especially thrushes) enjoy the female plants' fruit. This aromatic tree reaches 80 feet and thrives in moist, acidic soil in a mostly sunny spot. Transplanting can be tough, so avoid jostling the sapling's taproot when transferring to the ground. Pull out volunteers that sprout from seed to discourage a colony from forming.

Spice Bush

Lindera benzoin • Zones 4 to 9
The namesake of spicebush swallowtails, spice bush is also a host plant for the related eastern tiger butterfly. In spring, aromatic star-shaped green-yellow flowers appear, followed by red berries (on female plants) that are prized by songbirds. This woodland shrub grows up to 10 feet tall and wide and is an ideal candidate for a partly sunny spot that needs some interest, especially in autumn.

Tulip Tree

Liriodendron tulipifera
Zones 5 to 9
Though hard to see from afar, the tulip tree's spring to early-summer flowers will dress up your yard. The cup-shaped blooms have light-yellow petals with orange bases. Grosbeaks, finches and others eat the seeds. Be patient: Most types won't begin to flower for 10 to 12 years. But you won't have to wait for wildlife: Birds favor the tree for nesting, and it's a host for eastern tiger swallowtail caterpillars. This columnar tree can reach up to 100 feet tall.

Weigela

Weigela spp. • Zones 3 to 9
In addition to its pretty, trumpet-shaped late-spring flowers, which entice returning hummingbirds, weigela boasts attractive foliage throughout the growing season. In some varieties, leaves change color in fall. Sizes range from 2 to 8 feet tall and wide.

Wild Black Cherry

Prunus serotina • Zones 4 to 8
Popular among caterpillars—such as blues, hairstreaks and admirals—that munch on its leaf and flower buds, the wild black cherry's fruit is also sought after by birds later in the year. This fast-growing tree shines in fall, when its leaves turn yellow or red. It prefers some sun and is salt and drought tolerant.

Red Buckeye

Tulip Tree

Sassafras

Weigela

Spice Bush

Wild Black Cherry

GLORIOUS SPRING WILDLIFE *gardens*

Start the year right with one of these springtime planting plans.

Want to know the secret to spotting spring migrators? Fill your gardens with the flowers, shrubs and trees they seek. Not only will these planting plans increase your chances of seeing a warbler or a bunting, they'll encourage year-round residents to make a home in your yard, too.

Shady Show-Offs

Infuse a sun-starved spot with color, texture and life. Birds and butterflies value these plants for nourishment and shelter.

1. **Flowering dogwood** *Cornus florida*, Zones 5 to 8
2. **Lungwort** *Pulmonaria* spp., Zones 2 to 8
3. **Rhododendron** *Rhododendron* spp., Zones 4 to 10
4. **Columbine** *Aquilegia* spp., Zones 3 to 9
5. **Fern** varieties include *Polystichum* spp. and *Blechum* spp., Zones 2 to 10
6. **Hosta** *Hosta* spp., Zones 3 to 8

SWEET TREAT.
A black-chinned hummingbird stops to drink at a columbine.

Sweet Blossoms

Give passing fliers plenty of reasons to stick around with this group of late-spring all-stars.

1. **Dwarf mugo pine** *Pinus mugo*, Zones 2 to 7
2. **French lilac** *Syringa vulgaris*, Zones 3 to 8
3. **Dianthus** *Dianthus* spp., Zones 3 to 10
4. **Bergenia** *Bergenia cordifolia*, Zones 3 to 8
5. **Creeping thyme** *Thymus polytrichus*, Zones 5 to 9

No fence? **Mirror this garden plan**: Purchase extra perennials and plant them on the other side of the shrubs. It's a stand-alone showpiece!

our readers share

Which springtime birds and butterflies do you notice in your garden?

"I see chipping sparrows, an occasional goldfinch, and my perennial bluebirds, cardinals, mockers and house finches. I am lucky to see a spring azure, monarch or Carolina satyr along with early swallowtails, buckeyes, red-spotted purples and red admirals. Last spring I saw a falcate orangetip for the first time."

—SYBIL C., *Hemingway, SC*

"I see monarch butterflies here in New York! They are so beautiful when they spread their wings."

—IVY STELLA O., *via Facebook*

"We've had hummingbirds, scarlet tanagers, goldfinches, downy and hairy woodpeckers, robins, blue jays, indigo buntings, rose-breasted grosbeaks, red-winged blackbirds, chipping sparrows, Lincoln sparrows, orioles, but very few butterflies until early summer at my place."

—CAROL L., *Albert Lea, MN*

"Here in Bucks County, Pennsylvania, we have many. Of course, they are attracted to our plantings, feeders and birdhouses. We get monarchs, yellow and black swallowtails, wrens, robins, woodpeckers, blue jays, finches, cardinals, sparrows and many different kinds of bees."

—JACK B., *Levittown, PA*

"We have such a great variety in the Pacific Northwest! But my favorites are hummingbirds, chickadees and finches, robins and flickers. We are so lucky!"

—SUSIE O., *Bothell, WA*

STUNNING SPRING
containers

You don't have to wait for your garden beds to wake up to warmer weather. Perk up any outdoor space with a potted blend of blooms that your favorite fliers love.

High Five

Here's a cold-tolerant mix that's just as hardy as it is pretty.

LIGHT REQUIREMENTS: Part to full sun

POT SIZE: 14 inches

INGREDIENTS:

A. Winter Joy wallflower ~ 2 plants

B. Helena's Blush wood spurge 1 plant

C. Amethyst Myst coral bells 1 plant

D. Foamflower ~ 2 plants

E. Etain viola ~ 1 plant

A	A	B
D		D
C		E

Garden of Virtues

This planter will look and smell lovely for many springs to come: It showcases two shrubs!

LIGHT REQUIREMENT: Sun

POT SIZE: 24 inches

INGREDIENTS:

A. Bloomerang® Purple reblooming lilac ~ 1 plant

B. Bangle® dyers greenwood ~ 2 plants

Always Sunny

Infuse your landscape with a splash of cheery yellow and bright white—hues that happen to be beloved by butterflies and moths.

LIGHT REQUIREMENT: Sun

POT SIZE: 24 inches

INGREDIENTS:

A. Lemon Zest wallflower ~ 4 plants

B. Evergreen candytuft ~ 4 plants

C. Spring Silver mum ~ 2 plants

D. Pansy ~ 4 plants

Fancy-Free

Complementary pastels will surely sweeten up this season's often dreary landscape.

LIGHT REQUIREMENT: Sun

POT SIZE: 14 inches

INGREDIENTS:

A. Superbells® Peach calibrachoa ~ 2 plants

B. Laguna™ Sky Blue lobelia ~ 2 plants

C. Sunsatia® Lemon nemesia ~ 2 plants

Bold Beginnings

Bring primary colors to your spring palette with this trio of wildlife favorites.

LIGHT REQUIREMENT: Sun

POT SIZE: 12 inches

INGREDIENTS:

A. Butterfly marguerite daisy ~ 1 plant

B. Superbells® Red calibrachoa ~ 2 plants

C. Icterina golden leaf sage ~ 1 plant

String of Pearls

These early bloomers look lovely in any container, from a classic pot to a hanging basket—even a wall sconce.

LIGHT REQUIREMENT: Sun

POT SIZE: 14 inches

INGREDIENTS:

A. Variegatus dwarf white sweet flag ~ 1 plant

B. White Sequins™ rock cress ~ 4 plants

C. Polar™ White English daisy ~ 2 plants

Pure Enchantment

Dripping with springtime romance, this blend of flowers and foliage is anything but ordinary.

LIGHT REQUIREMENT: Sun

POT SIZE: 24 inches

INGREDIENTS:

A. Polar™ Pink English daisy ~ 2 plants

B. Autumn Glory bergenia ~ 1 plant

C. Helena's Blush wood spurge ~ 1 plant

D. Ribbon grass ~ 1 plant

E. Foamflower ~ 1 plant

spring BIRDING *basics*

WHO'S THERE?
Look for these birds in your yard.

YELLOW EXPLOSION: The American goldfinch is dull in color all winter but molts in the spring, growing new bright-yellow feathers. Come late March or April, your finch feeder suddenly becomes loaded with vivid yellow birds. Keep your thistle fresh and full to make these colorful fliers happy. And if your feeder is always crowded, think about adding a second one to bring in even more finches!

TERRIFIC TANAGERS: The stunning red-and-yellow western tanager in the West, scarlet tanager in the East and blazing summer tanager in the South all might visit your birdbath or even your suet feeder during their spring migration, but don't expect to see them for long. Insect- and fruit-loving tanagers are secretive during nesting, so be on the lookout!

SPRINGTIME SWEET TOOTH: Watch for orioles and hummingbirds to return in search of high-energy sweets to eat. Because flowers can be scarce before early May, these nectar-loving migrants will readily come to sugar-water feeders. I've even seen orioles clinging to a hanging geranium basket and plucking the nectar-rich blossoms.

THE USUAL SUSPECTS: Don't ignore your regular customers. Seed-eating house finches, chickadees, nuthatches, jays and cardinals, along with suet-loving woodpeckers, hang around all year. Small flocks of chickadees and nuthatches begin to disperse as we get closer to nesting season.

WHAT'S ON THE MENU?
Give birds what they need.

SLIM PICKIN'S: Don't stop feeding the birds just because it's warming up a bit. Less natural food is available to your birds in the early spring than at any other time of year. Most berries and seeds from shrubs, trees and flowers have been eaten throughout the winter, and minimal new growth has begun. It's also too early for most insects, so your backyard visitors have little to eat.

Suet is an important food in spring, when **natural food is scarce**. You'll be surprised whom it attracts!

These seasonal pointers will help you bring more birds to your yard.

BY ANNE SCHMAUSS

A STEADY DIET: Backyard songbirds will continue to eat a good-quality seed blend loaded with black-oil sunflower throughout the year, and spring is no exception. Also, suet eaters, including woodpeckers, enjoy a tasty snack in spring. High-fat food should still be on the menu.

SPRINGTIME BUFFET: Fresh orange halves can lure orioles to your backyard and might even tempt tanagers, grosbeaks and house finches. Apple halves can also attract birds like cardinals and woodpeckers. Put out mealworms to entice insect eaters like bluebirds and robins.

SONGBIRDS AND SUET: Many think of suet as a winter treat for woodpeckers, but it's also a secret weapon for attracting springtime migrants like warblers, tanagers and kinglets. Use a fatty suet loaded with nuts, berries and calcium. Secure your feeder flush against a shrub or tree so birds like warblers can comfortably eat. The branches will provide protection should a predator threaten.

IN A NUTSHELL
These quick hints are just in time!

SAFETY GLASS: Place static-cling decals on the outside of your windows to keep spring migrants from crashing into the glass. Spring and fall, when so many birds are on the move, are when songbirds are most likely to be injured from window strikes.

BIRD MAGNET: Install a birdbath and you'll double the variety of birds that visit. Not all birds eat seed or suet, but they all need water every day. Lure migrating songbirds with the sight and sound of moving water. Adding a small fountain or a bubbler will turn the bath into an irresistible bird magnet.

HOUSE HUNTING: Spring is prime house hunting time for birds, but not all houses are a good fit for every species. Chickadees, for instance, require a house with specific dimensions. Ask at a nearby backyard-bird store which houses are suitable for your local birds, or find our birdhouse guidelines at *birdsandblooms.com*.

SPRING FEVER. It's time for birds such as male goldfinches (far left) and western tanagers (near left) to show off bright new plumage. Plus, watch for migrators, like Baltimore orioles (center) and indigo buntings (above). Year-round favorites, including downy woodpeckers (top), will keep as active as ever.

YEAR-ROUND *butterflies:* SPRING

Keep an eye out for these early fliers.
BY **KENN KAUFMAN**

Spring's arrival is hard to pin down on a calendar, but all over North America, butterflies mark the unfolding season.

Springtime Specialties

In the southernmost U.S., winter fades almost imperceptibly into spring. Elsewhere, however, particular butterflies are sure signs of springtime: They don't fly at any other time of year. Among these are small white butterflies such as West Virginia and spring whites, and various types of orangetips and marbles. Their caterpillars feed on wild plants in the mustard family, which grow mainly in spring. The adult butterflies must emerge early so females can lay eggs and the caterpillars can feed while the plants are available.

Other spring specialties include certain tiny blue butterflies, such as the spring azure and the silvery blue. These little gems may show up in gardens or gather by the dozens around the edges of mud puddles. Less noticeable are some small, dark hairstreaks and skippers—somewhat obscure, but worth seeking out for their poetic names, like frosted elfin or sleepy duskywing. But no one is likely to overlook some of the big swallowtails that start flying early in the season, such as the gorgeous streamer-winged zebra swallowtail.

Returning North

Early in spring, monarch butterflies that have wintered in Mexico will begin to move north, eventually crossing into Texas. At some point, the females will stop and lay eggs on milkweed plants, launching another generation to continue the journey. Before the end of May, the vanguard of migrants will reach the Great Lakes or even southern Canada.

A few others—red admirals, painted ladies and American ladies among them—are on the move, too, though not in such a well-organized or predictable way. In the Southwest, tens of thousands of painted ladies may take part in a mass flight, flooding into gardens along their path.

Week by week, new nonmigratory butterflies emerge: bright sulphurs, subtle satyrs, flashy fritillaries and others add to the color palette that will grace summer gardens.

Painted Lady

GLAD YOU ASKED

Our resident plant, bird and butterfly experts welcome your springtime wildlife-garden questions.

Educate yourself! **Find out what species are invasive in your area.** Visit *invasivespeciesinfo.gov* in the U.S. and *ec.gc.ca* in Canada for local resources.

GROWING UP FAST

I planted this tree (left) when it was a little over a foot high. Now, it's about 15 to 20 feet tall, and to my delight, it produces beautiful blooms in the spring. **The hummingbirds and insects love it. Can you tell me more?**

—ALETTA B., *Murrieta, CA*

MELINDA MYERS: This fast-growing tree goes by a few common names, including empress tree, princess tree or royal paulownia (its botanical name is *Paulownia tomentosa*). As you know, it is very beautiful while in bloom, but it's also named as an invasive plant in some regions.

Its adaptable nature helped this tree naturalize in the eastern U.S. and on the West Coast more than 150 years ago. As a native to China, this tree was cultivated for medicinal, ornamental and ceremonial purposes. It's probably a good idea to find out if the tree is considered a nuisance in your area.

SAVE THE TREES

We have several birch, mountain ash and willow trees that are dying as a result of sapsuckers. **They drill holes in the bark (below), sometimes encircling the entire tree. Can we stop the birds without harming them?**

—JANET L,. *Smelterville, ID*

GEORGE HARRISON: Red-naped and Williamson's sapsuckers could be the perpetrators, since both of these birds spend their breeding season in Idaho.

These birds tend to focus on specific species of trees, so if all of your trees are dying, sapsuckers may not be the cause. Overall, they drill on trees to make the sap flow. This may appear to be detrimental, but the shallow holes rarely kill the tree.

To protect your trees, try surrounding the trunks with fine wire or netting.

MELINDA: Sapsuckers will feed on a variety of trees but prefer the sap of pines, spruces, birch and fruit trees.

As George points out, their feeding seldom kills a tree. Repeated sapsucker attacks, however, can weaken the tree and the feeding holes can create entryways for insects and disease. If the problem continues, you can also try wrapping the tree trunk with burlap, which should encourage the birds to dine elsewhere.

 Turn the page for more expert advice!

HOME SWEET HOME?

I have two butterfly houses, but I'm not sure where to hang them. Do these **houses really attract butterflies?**

—DONNA H., *Pendleton, IN*

TOM ALLEN: Butterfly houses are more of a garden decoration than a way to attract butterflies to your yard.

Although a few butterfly species seek shelter for winter hibernation or a shady roost during the summer, most butterflies usually rest on vegetation or in trees.

However, if you put your houses in a protected area near woodlands, you could attract a mourning cloak or question mark. And in areas where Milbert's tortoiseshells are found, a butterfly house might be effective, since these butterflies hibernate in large groups.

Be aware, however, that butterfly houses also make good homes for wasps and hornets.

ABANDONED NEST

I saw just one bluebird enter my bluebird house in the spring. In May, I noticed a sheet of moss was covering the floor. After two weeks, I took it out so other birds could use the house. **Five small eggs were embedded in it.** What made this nest?

—RACHEL S., *Maple Hill, NC*

GEORGE: The moss and eggs in the house are those of a Carolina chickadee, which will often nest in a bluebird house. As I write, I have a chickadee nesting in a bluebird house in my backyard. It laid down a floor of moss, and then placed fur and hair on top.

READY TO GET GROWING

We live in a new house on a virtually empty lot. What are some **fast-growing plants that will attract birds** and other wildlife?

—ANONYMOUS

MELINDA: A mix of annuals, perennials, trees and shrubs will provide the food and shelter that wildlife need.

Annuals offer immediate results in any flower garden. Here are some that do well in most soil conditions: sunflower, dahlia, marigold, zinnia, verbena, nasturtium, petunia and cleome.

For perennials, choose yarrow, hollyhock, pearly everlasting, rock cress, butterfly weed, coneflower, black-eyed Susan, daylily, phlox, lupine, bee balm or sedum. They'll start filling in and blooming the second year.

Then add evergreens and deciduous trees and shrubs like dogwood, viburnum, shrub rose, hawthorn and maple.

BUTTERFLY DELIGHT

My backyard butterflies love this flower (right). **The blooms smell like carnations** and don't last long. Can you tell me more?

—JULIE D., *Tallahassee, FL*

MELINDA: Plant identification by photo is often challenging. I count on my experience, visits to gardens, fellow experts and arboreta across the country for help. In this case, I consulted *Birds & Blooms* butterfly expert, Tom Allen.

He confirmed the plant is a pinxterbloom azalea (*Rhododendron periclymenoides*). This low-growing azalea produces runners and lots of branches. It typically grows anywhere from 2 to 10 feet tall, and the fragrant flowers appear in spring. Tolerant of sandy, dry and rocky soils, this azalea is hardy in Zones 4 to 8.

When featuring **used auto parts in your garden**, clean them well!

A ROCK THE BOAT
Make a splash with a large-scale addition to your garden decor. "This small boat was too tippy for the water, and our friends were happy to get rid of it. I turned it into a planter," Evelyn Norris from Rainy Lake, Ontario, tells us. "It's easy to weed and water, and it's a real conversation piece," she says.

BACKYARD BUILDERS

Just in time for Earth Day, get inspired by these clever readers who gave old junk new life.

< FLOWER POWER
Jack Horoho of North Manchester, Indiana, puts an original spin on wildlife gardening. "I made this red dwelling from a clay pot, with a license plate for a roof," he says. "The best thing about my houses is that they're simple so anyone can make them!"

A HUBCAP FEEDER
Here's an industrial-strength idea from Chris and Scott Peterson of Barrington, New Jersey: Make a feeder from a hubcap. "Replace the seed regularly to prevent mold, especially after it rains or snows," suggests Chris, who sells these feeders and others at *starlingink.com*.

< A LIGHT IN THE DARK
Edward Roach of Carriere, Mississippi, really did turn trash to treasure with this project. While removing debris after Hurricane Katrina, his wife, Mary, rescued a sconce from the garbage and placed it on his workbench. "I removed all the wiring and painted the panes yellow on three sides. I replaced the front one with plywood for the entrance hole," he says. "Now the 'Katrina House' is a great home for feathered friends."

< BIRD-THEMED BAFFLE
"This wild birdseed canister ended up being the perfect squirrel and chipmunk deterrent," says Cedarburg, Wisconsin, reader Sally Bresler. "My husband simply adapted the container to fit around our feeder post. After that, the squirrels and chipmunks didn't stand a chance!"

SPRING PROJECTS

If you have something that will work as roofing material but you don't like the look of it, **paint it with glue and press sheet moss over it.** It provides a gorgeous green roof, and the birds love pulling out bits of moss for their nests!

bluebird
B&B

This one-of-a-kind nesting box doubles as a mealworm feeder.

BY ALISON AUTH

You'll love this fresh take on the classic bluebird abode—and so will they.

THIS BED-AND-BREAKFAST DESIGN offers a fun alternative to ordinary bluebird houses. To make it yourself, just buy or build a plain bluebird nest box and dress it up to make an attractive B&B. Pretty soon, you'll be singing a little "Zip-a-dee-doo-dah" in your own backyard.

Whether you buy a basic bluebird house or decide to make your own, there are a few necessities. First, make sure it has ventilation holes at the top, drainage holes in the bottom and a clean-out door for annual maintenance. The house should have a 5-by-5-inch floor, a height of 8 to 12 inches and an entrance hole of 1-1/2 inches placed 6 to 10 inches above the floor. Mount the house 5 to 10 feet above the ground toward an open field on a fence, post, utility pole or tree.

Use your imagination, and you'll have a B&B no bluebird could resist!

1. The box. Old columns cut to size make for easy birdhouse building. All they need is a roof, a bottom, a door and whatever adornments tickle your fancy. I frequently visit our local architectural salvage yard, where I load my wagon with a column or two, skeleton keys, old door hardware and cabinet knobs, hooks of all shapes and sizes, orphaned light canopies and other assorted castaways. If you don't have a column lying around, don't fret. Four pieces of wood cut to size and nailed together will put you in business.

2. The roof. As a fan of Dr. Seuss illustrations, I find that many of my box designs are curvy and whimsical. The roof of this house, which uses tin flashing, is an example. I've provided a pattern (available to download at *birdsandblooms.com*) in case you'd like to duplicate it, but there are much easier ways to build a roof! Any kind of flexible, water-impervious material can be used to cover a wood substrate. Rubber, Sunbrella fabric scraps, tin, copper and aluminum flashing all work.

3. The clean-out door. I like to cut out my doors before I put the bottom on the house. I use a jigsaw, but you can also do it with an old-fashioned coping saw. Hinge the door with a little strip of rubber or fabric, or a little metal hinge, as I've done here.

4. The base. Before I attach my base to the house, I prefer to attach "feet" or a pedestal to the base. Even though I'll be mounting the house on a fence, I can never resist adding them anyway. I just like the way they look. If you do, too, you can use anything from old coat hooks (which remind me of bird feet) to sticks from the yard, antique ceiling light canopies, tub faucet handles, candlestick bases or even small discarded lamp bases. Start wandering around your garage or rifle through your junk drawers. You never know what you might find that will work perfectly! I used an old piano leg for my house here, with the idea that the house could be mounted on the post from the base or the back.

5. Perches and predator guards. Perches right in front of the entrance hole can pose a real threat to baby birds and eggs. Predators use them to extend their reach into the house, so put a perch on the side of the house. Here, I attached a wrought-iron plant holder to double as a side perch and a convenient place to leave food. A predator guard can be anything applied to the entrance hole to add depth. I've used radiator and plumbing supply escutcheons, porcelain light sockets and even a block of wood with the same diameter hole drilled in it and nailed over the existing hole. Anything that makes it harder for a squirrel or raccoon paw to reach inside the house will do.

6. Finishing touches. This is the fun part! Paint and adornments of all kinds can make your house one of a kind. (Whether you paint or not, remember to use a top coat of clear shellac sealer.) The wrought-iron plant holder on the side of my house, for instance, presents several options. You can use it for a live plant, or turn it into a feeder for bluebirds and fill it with mealworms.

WHAT YOU NEED

- Bluebird house (or wood or recycled material if you want to make your own)
- Base of your choice
- Roofing material of your choice
- Material for clean-out door, including hinge, handle, etc.
- Paint
- Clear shellac sealer
- Assorted screws and nails
- Cordless drill
- Drill bits
- Jigsaw or coping saw
- Tin snips
- Plant holder with a dish to fit

oriole WREATH

Simple and elegant, these little feeders will attract oodles of winged visitors.

BY ALISON AUTH

WHAT YOU NEED

Coat hanger

Needle-nose pliers (or strong hands)

Wire cutters

Oranges

Cutting board

Good kitchen knife for slicing

Ribbon and berries (optional)

I ENJOY THE BRIGHT SILHOUETTES of orioles in my window, especially after a long winter. They love fresh oranges and are also attracted to the color orange, making these wreaths the perfect enticement. Hang one near a sturdy branch so an oriole has a perch from which to peck!

1. Remove the cardboard tube from your hanger, if necessary, and bend the two sides of the hanger toward each other until they are spaced 1 inch apart.

2. Shape the outline of a bird, as shown. I found that using my hands was the easiest way to start. Then I used needle-nose pliers to shape and smooth any rough curves.

3. Use the pliers or a wire cutter to snip the curled ends off the hanger.

4. Cut oranges into about 1/4-inch slices. Then, cut little pieces of rind from the orange ends into roughly 1/2-inch triangles. These will function as spacers between the slices and help keep everything in place.

5. Thread an orange slice through both wires. Then thread a piece of rind next to it on one or both wires.

6. Repeat step No. 5, threading more of the orange slices, until you run out of wire.

7. Tie a little bow around the bird's "neck" and add some berries at the ends. Hang the feeder close to a window to see the orioles swoop in for a snack!

cup&saucer
FEEDER

Make a coffee date with the birds.

PROJECT AND PHOTOS BY
DAISY SISKIN

WHAT YOU NEED

Cup and saucer

Masking tape

Drill

3/8-inch masonry bit

Two 10 mm flat metal washers

One 3/8-inch threaded metal rod (these usually come in 6-foot lengths)

Exterior spray paint for metal

Hacksaw

Two rubber washers

One 3/8-inch stainless steel nut

One 3/8-inch stainless steel wing nut

For a bit of whimsy, **attach a teaspoon to the saucer** using an adhesive meant for ceramic and metal items.

a

b

I LOVE TO SIT AND REVIVE myself with a nice cup of coffee every now and then. The next time I take my morning brew out to the patio, I can lift a cup in salute as I share the experience with my avian neighbors.

I spent an afternoon thrift shopping and found just the right cup and saucer to complement some fine feathers. A trip to the hardware store provided everything needed to start on a new feeder project. Here's how I did it—and how you can, too!

1. Wearing safety glasses, carefully drill a hole through the center of your cup and another one through the saucer. To help center the drill bit while I started the hole, I secured a washer to the center of the piece with masking tape. This part takes some patience. Apply only gentle pressure to keep the piece from cracking. Earthenware is easier to drill through than stoneware.

2. Spray-paint the threaded rod your desired color. Paint the first few inches lightly to avoid filling in the threads. Allow to dry.

3. Choose the location of your feeder. Decide how far off the ground you want it to be. If protection from predators is an issue, the feeder should be at least 4 feet high. I cut 1 foot from the 6-foot rod with a hacksaw. Once you've cut the rod to length, push it into the ground.

4. Screw the nut about 2 inches onto the rod. Top with a metal washer, then a rubber washer. Place the saucer and then the cup onto the assembly through the holes you have drilled (**fig. a**). Inside the cup, add the second rubber washer, then the second metal washer. Last, gently tighten the wing nut to secure your feeder (**fig. b**).

5. Fill the cup with seeds for the birds and go put the coffee on for yourself. To remove the feeder for cleaning in the future, simply unscrew the wing nut and lift it off.

Duckling
Adrian Maull ~ Jacksonville, FL

Crocus Buds
Edward Peterson Jr. ~ Columbus, OH

Baltimore Oriole
Kristine Quandee ~ Joliet, IL

SPRING GARDEN
gallery

Watch the world awaken through the eyes
of shutterbugs—birders just like you!

Tulip Field
Timothy DeHan ~ Redmond, WA

House Finch
Larry Keller ~ Lititz, PA

Forsythia
Catherine Knight Voss ~ Gadsden, AL

Hooded Warbler
Pamela Johnson ~ Vicksburg, MS

Flowering Quince
C. C. Vermillion ~ Bryant, AR

Baby Wrens
Peggy Franz ~ Hillsboro, MO

Tulip
Carlee Grace ~ Erie, PA

Daffodils
Dr. Ira Tucker ~ Cary, NC

share your talents!

Want your photography or a story to be considered for *Birds & Blooms* publications? See our reader submission guidelines at *birdsandblooms.com*.

soaking in SUMMER

summer BACKYARD *checklist*

Stay on top of your chores this summer so you can spend more of your time relaxing in your bird-and-butterfly paradise!

Large and graceful, **swallowtails live all over the world**. There are more than 30 types in the U.S. and Canada.

THE AMAZING ZINNIA. Why are zinnias a must-have butterfly garden component? Let us count the ways: They're simple to grow from seed; easy to care for; bloom in many butterfly-approved hues; and last long into fall.

Entice Wildlife With Plants

☐ **ATTRACT** beneficial insects to your garden—along with the birds that eat them! Sweet alyssum, creeping thyme, veronica, bugleweed, lavender, yarrow and others attract lady beetles, lacewings, parasitic wasps and other insects that feed on garden pests.

☐ **HAVE** thistles in your garden? Stop yourself from pulling them out: American goldfinches (like the one above) wait for the thistles to mature and use the down to build their nests.

☐ **EXTEND** butterfly and hummingbird season by filling your garden with long-blooming nectar plants, such as zinnias (left), agastache and blanket flower.

☐ **DEADHEAD** salvias, snapdragons and other flowers that often stop blooming after the first go-round. Use sharp garden scissors or hand pruners to cut below the spent blossoms and above a set of leaves. This allows side shoots to flower and attract sought-after fliers.

With long summer days, there's no shortage of outdoor tasks to accomplish.

Here's a useful checklist so you can get your to-do's done ASAP. From simple garden care short cuts to ways to provide water for butterflies and hummingbirds, this list will help you make the most of summer.

Keep Your Eyes Peeled

☐ **MIGRATION** isn't just a fall event. It actually starts in late summer, so keep an eye out for warblers, some sparrows and other fliers as they head south for winter. Remember that not all birds will be in their typical spring plumage. Challenge yourself to ID the mystery fliers in your area.

☐ **THIS** is the season when many juveniles (like the Baltimore oriole at right) are out and about. Notice the slight differences between little ones and their parents.

☐ **HUNT** for nests in your backyard. Look at the forks of trees and in shrubs with dense foliage and branches to see if you can spot nests hidden inside.

Beckon Birds

☐ **MAKE** nectar for hummingbirds by mixing 4 parts water and 1 part white sugar. Heat can cause sugar water to ferment, so switch out the nectar in your feeder at least twice a week. Don't give up if hummers don't notice right away; it may take time.

☐ **NYJER** seed (also known as thistle) is definitely more expensive, but it's a real treat for finches. Buy it in bulk and store it in a cool, dry place.

☐ **BLUEBIRDS**, robins and many others love bugs. Try offering a dish of live or roasted mealworms to entice these insect eaters.

☐ **FREQUENTLY** replenish birdbath water in hot weather. Maintain a depth of no more than a couple of inches to allow birds to stand while bathing.

☐ **ATTRACT** even more hummingbirds by putting your garden hose on a mist setting. They love water and will bathe in it.

Bring in the Butterflies

☐ **CREATE** butterfly feeding areas in shady spots with fruit, such as melon pieces, or small sponges soaked with a sports drink. But keep in mind that in the summer heat, these feeders can get moldy, so tend to yours regularly.

☐ **SUMMER** is peak time for many insect pests in the garden, such as the Japanese beetle (right). Be careful about using pesticides, because they seriously affect butterflies and other beneficial insects.

☐ **JOIN** a butterfly organization in your area. Find out if they participate in the annual North American butterfly count.

☐ **IF** your garden has a water feature, it can do double duty as a birdbath. Place a few large rocks around the edge to give butterflies and birds a convenient place to sit and drink.

SWALLOWTAIL: CONNIE ETTER; GOLDFINCH: PAUL BROWN JR., BABY ORIOLE: DORI SMITH; BEETLE: BRUCE MACQUEEN / SHUTTERSTOCK.COM

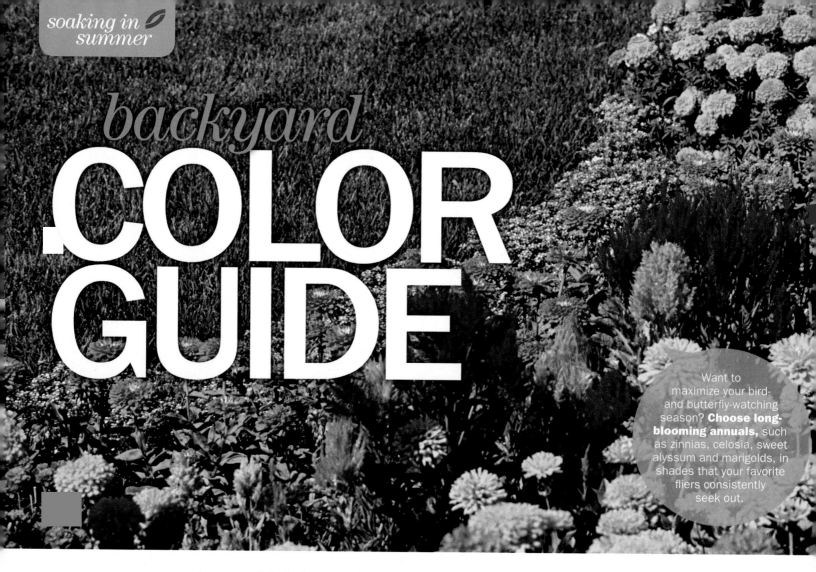

backyard COLOR GUIDE

Want to maximize your bird- and butterfly-watching season? **Choose long-blooming annuals,** such as zinnias, celosia, sweet alyssum and marigolds, in shades that your favorite fliers consistently seek out.

Learn which hues will attract wildlife to your garden. BY SALLY ROTH

POLLINATION POINTER.
Color is just one part of the pollination puzzle. Fragrance and form count as well, but color is the element most gardeners notice first.

It seems as if I'm always fiddling with my flowers, prying out the flaming-red azalea that's in the wrong spot, or moving a clump of wild columbines clear across the yard.

Rearranging is half the fun of gardening for me, but hummers don't give a whit about the beauty of our gardens. To them, flowers are nothing but food.

When I shift their favorites, such as that azalea and those columbines, I'm moving their dinner plate. Come spring, they'll be hovering at the plants' old location, just as they do when I'm a bit late getting their feeder back into its place.

Luckily, no matter how often we rearrange our plants, there's a major clue that shows hummingbirds and other nectar-seeking garden visitors where the food is—color.

The Birds and the Bees

We all know that hummingbirds can't resist investigating the color red. Whether it's a plastic feeder, a tall stem of a canna or a dab of bright lipstick, the tiny birds zoom to the hue.

Almost all flowers that depend on hummers for pollination are red or orange-red. Their nectar is held deep inside a long tube, where it's inaccessible to other pollinators. No wonder hummers zero in on red—a sweet payoff is practically guaranteed.

This isn't the case for bees. Bumblebees, mason bees and our other buzzy friends see the ultraviolet spectrum. To their eyes, vivid red hummingbird flowers simply blend into the background. It's hues of blue that inspire a beeline—especially deep blue and blue-purple.

understanding color

DULL RED: A & J VISAGE / ALAMY

Boost your butterflies, tempt more hummers or bring in the bees by planting more of their favorite colors.

WHITE OR PALE COLOR

ATTRACTS: Night-flying moths; bats, in some areas
FLOWERS: Moonflower, angel's trumpet (*Datura* or *Brugmansia*), white or pale-hued petunias, evening primrose

YELLOW

ATTRACTS: Butterflies
FLOWERS: Sunflowers, black-eyed Susans, gaillardia, marigolds, golden alyssum

PURPLE

ATTRACTS: Butterflies
FLOWERS: Butterfly bush, coneflower, asters, verbenas, Russian sage, petunias, lavender, candytuft, agastache, azaleas, rhododendrons

RED OR ORANGE

ATTRACTS: Hummingbirds
FLOWERS: Scarlet honeysuckle, bee balm, columbines, canna, gladiolus, lilies, salvias, trumpet vine, ocotillo, azaleas

BLUE TO BLUE-PURPLE

ATTRACTS: Bees
FLOWERS: Crocus, hyacinth, grape hyacinth, salvias, agastache, blue spirea, campanulas

DULL RED OR RED-BROWN

ATTRACTS: Flies
FLOWERS: Wild ginger, Dutchman's pipe vine, trilliums, pawpaw trees and some arums, including skunk cabbage; another in this group is *Rafflesia arnoldii* (shown), the world's largest flower, which boosts fly appeal with a fetid odor that you probably don't want in your yard!

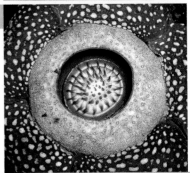

Butterflies and Other Insects

While bees get the blues, butterflies wing their way to purple and yellow. Countless flowers in those colors offer a secure perch where butterflies can sit and sip to their hearts' content.

Maybe you'd rather have flies? Dull-red or red-brown blooms will do the trick. They mimic rotting flesh to lure their pollinators.

Pollination doesn't stop at sunset. White or pale flowers attract moths (and bats in the desert Southwest) after other blooms have disappeared in the dark. Sit beneath an arbor of moonflower vine (*Ipomoea alba*), and you'll likely spot a sphinx moth hovering at the snowy blossoms.

BEYOND
butterflies

Lay out the welcome mat for these beneficial insects.

STORY AND PHOTOS BY **BILL JOHNSON**

**Twelve-Spotted
Skimmer Dragonfly**

When we think of beneficial insects in the garden, butterflies are usually at the top of the list. However, if we could take a bug census, we would discover that butterflies make up one of the smallest percentages of all insects visiting our yards.

From dragonflies to bees, hundreds of insects frequent our backyards. And while a handful are considered pests, most play a helpful role or are at least completely harmless.

In my own backyard, we leave a small part of our lawn wild to create a natural habitat for our insect visitors. In turn, we attract a wide variety of crawlers, fliers and hoppers that pollinate our flowers, gather nectar and eat pesky bugs. In addition, they enhance the garden experience with their beautiful colors or sounds.

While specific insects vary greatly by region, here are a few that you actually want to see in your yard. Go ahead—venture out to your garden so you can take a closer look. You just might be amazed at what you find.

Widow Skimmer Dragonfly

Green Darner Dragonfly

dragonflies

Twelve-Spotted Skimmer Dragonfly

Libellula pulchella • wingspan: 3 inches

You'll notice these dragonflies throughout summer, flying over gardens looking for food. Because they—and all dragonflies—have multifaceted eyes, they are extremely good hunters and eat all sorts of other insects, especially mosquitoes.

Widow Skimmer Dragonfly

Libellula luctuosa • wingspan: 3 inches

You can often spot this common dragonfly perched on the tip of a branch, staking out a territory for hunting. They will chase off other dragonflies and eat mosquitoes and many other insects. The white patches on the wings and the pale-blue abdomen identify this one as a male. The female has no white on her wings, and her abdomen is brown with orange stripes on the sides.

Green Darner Dragonfly

Anax junius • wingspan: 4+ inches

These are our largest dragonflies. Very strong fliers, they're one of the best insect-eaters in our gardens. Green darners start their lives as nymphs in water and emerge as winged adults. Nymphs eat mosquito larvae, and the adults eat the mosquitoes that bite us.

Red Milkweed Beetle

Milkweed Leaf Beetle

Pennsylvania Leatherwing Beetle

Bumble Bee

Virescent Green Metallic Bee

Honeybee

beetles

Red Milkweed Beetle

Tetraopes tetrophthalmus • 1/2 inch

If there are any milkweeds in your yard, this beetle will show up, especially if you grow common milkweed, its favorite host plant. Its bright-red color warns birds and other insects, "Don't eat me. I'm toxic."

Milkweed Leaf Beetle

Labidomera clivicollis • 3/8 inch

This distinctly colored beetle is common in gardens where milkweed has been allowed to grow. Often mistaken for ladybugs, they're almost twice the size.

Pennsylvania Leatherwing Beetle

Chauliognathus pennsylvanicus • 5/8 inch

Common in gardens and considered beneficial, these beetles transfer pollen between flowers, plus they eat aphids and other insect pests. If you grow goldenrod or Joe Pye weed, you'll very likely see them on those plants.

bees

Bumble Bee

Bombus spp. • 3/4 inch

One of the most entertaining insects in the garden, it's a rather clumsy flier and stays on flowers such as bee balm and coneflowers long enough for you to take a picture. You can see the pollen sacs on its hind legs. A very beneficial pollinator, the bumble bee is capable of stinging, but will only do so if it feels threatened.

Virescent Green Metallic Bee

Agapostemon virescens • 1/2 inch

You'll see this bee in most gardens. A shiny green metallic head and thorax and banded abdomen clearly make the virescent green metallic bee stand out from other fliers. This bee, which is a pollinator, makes its nest in the ground.

Honeybee

Apis mellifera • 5/8 inch

Besides producing the honey that we eat, honeybees serve as major pollinators. They're known as social insects because they live in large colonies. Although they're capable of stinging, they will do so only when they feel threatened.

Leafcutter Bee

Megachile latimanus • 1/2 inch

Although sometimes mistaken for honeybees, the markings on their abdomens identify these as leafcutter bees. Considered solitary bees, they live alone in nests in the ground. Beneficial as pollinators, they also eat small caterpillars. Unlike honeybees, leafcutter bees have no pollen sacs on their legs. Instead, rows of hairs under their abdomens gather and distribute the pollen as they fly from flower to flower.

Bee Fly

Long-Legged Fly

Flower Fly

Green Lacewing

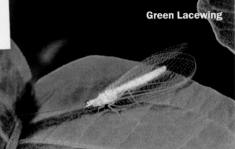

flies

Bee Fly

Poecilanthrax spp. • 1/2 inch

This flier gets its name because it resembles a furry bee. What looks like a stinger going into the flower is actually a proboscis (tongue) used to gather nectar. It's harmless, can't sting and is a beneficial pollinator.

Long-Legged Fly

Condylostylus spp. • 1/4 inch

Watch for these common flies racing around on leaves. They eat aphids, mites and other small insects. Their metallic colors—in green, bronze, blue or gold—make them easy to see when sunlight hits them.

Flower Fly

Helophilus fasciatus • 5/8 inch

These flies help control aphids, especially their larvae. They also pollinate by flying among flowers. As part of their self-defense, several types are good bee mimics with coloration that looks quite similar to bees. But because they're flies, they can't really sting.

other beneficial bugs

Green Lacewing

Chrysopa spp. • 1/2 inch

This beautiful insect is very common and very beneficial. Its larvae eat as many aphids as they can find. You'll see it in the garden during the day and near light sources at night.

Broad-Winged Katydid

Microcentrum rhombifolium • 2 inches

Katydids are a frequent evening sight near light sources. The night calls of the adults are part of the sunset symphony throughout the summer into fall.

Snowy Tree Cricket

Oecanthus fultoni • 3/4 inch

You probably haven't seen these, but you've definitely heard them. In late summer and into the fall, the chirping you hear in the evening comes from snowy tree crickets. They're not very big, but they make quite a racket.

Great Spangled
Fritillary

SUMMER PLANTS

*birds &
butterflies
love*

**Hoping for more
friendly fliers in
your yard? Count
on these flowers,
trees and shrubs.**

During the summer, the list of backyard bloomers is practically endless. So why not make the decision a little easier on yourself by choosing plants that enhance your landscape and attract winged wildlife? Here, we offer more than 50 plants that do just that, and they're all at their peak this season.

annuals, biennials & perennials

Agastache
Agastache spp. • Zones 5 to 11
Bushy and studded with blooms from mid- to late summer, agastache is a favorite of hummingbirds, butterflies and bees. Flower spires in violet, orange, yellow, pink or blue reach 2 to 6 feet high. Agastache thrives in full sun and in well-draining, fertile soil.

Bachelor's Button
Centaurea cyanus • annual
Growing best in full sun, bachelor's button comes in several colors, including blue, pink, red, white and purple. Though considered an annual, its seeds ensure a new crop each year. Butterflies will visit for nectar, and in fall, finches, buntings and sparrows will stop by to nibble from the seed heads. Also known as cornflower, this charmer is long-lasting when cut and holds its color when dried.

Baptisia
Baptisia spp. • Zones 3 to 9
In early summer, this North American native's stems are laden with small flowers that later form structural seed heads sought after by birds. Select from a variety of colors, cultivars and hybrids to find the perfect plant for your space. Plant baptisia with ample room in a place where you won't have to move it: It develops a deep taproot and is finicky about being transplanted.

Bee Balm
Monarda spp. • Zones 3 to 9
Also known as bergamot, this unusual beauty grows up to 4 feet tall and starts flowering in midsummer, inviting hummingbirds, butterflies and bees to your flower bed. Plants come in hues of pink, red, white and purple; choose mildew-resistant varieties for best results. Frequent deadheading will keep this enthusiastic self-sower in check, but then you won't see songbirds stopping to eat the seeds once petals die back. The choice is yours!

Blanket Flower
Gaillardia spp. • Zones 3 to 10
Not only is blanket flower bright and cheery, it's one tough plant. Tolerant of drought and a variety of soil conditions, this North American native, sometimes grown as an annual, is a standout in any sunny spot. At the end of the growing season, you can save and dry the seeds and plant them the following spring.

Blazing Star
Liatris spp. • Zones 3 to 9
The nectar of this spiky plant is a butterfly favorite, especially when it comes to the silver-spotted skipper. After the flowers fade, birds favor the seeds, which are easy to pick out in the garden: Plants reach up to 6 feet tall! Some types, like Kobold, are much shorter, measuring roughly 18 inches.

Agastache

Bee Balm

Bachelor's Button

Blanket Flower

Baptisia

Blazing Star

Butterfly Weed

Asclepias tuberosa • Zones 3 to 9
Not solely a treat for butterflies, this drought-tolerant plant is a wildlife garden must-have. Its foliage is the food of larval monarch and queen butterflies, while hummingbirds love the flat-topped flower clusters' nectar and birds, such as goldfinches and orioles, use the silky down of spent seed pods as nesting material. Despite its name, it's far from being a pest.

Calibrachoa

Calibrachoa spp. • annual
Its small petunialike flowers will steal the show all season, making fast-growing calibrachoa a hot choice for beds and containers—especially those that are geared toward butterflies and hummingbirds. Use it as a nicely textured filler plant or as a bold stand-alone. Plants reach about 8 inches tall and spread to about 1 foot wide.

Cardinal Flower

Lobelia cardinalis • Zones 3 to 9
A moisture-loving favorite, bright-red cardinal flower grows 3 to 5 feet tall and blooms for most of summer and into autumn. It does well when planted in full sun to partial shade and fertile, moist soil. Hummingbirds and butterflies (especially those in the swallowtail family) seek out this plant's nectar, but don't expect to see cardinals hanging around nearby: The flower is named merely for the color.

Cleome

Cleome hassleriana • annual
Plant this tropical native in your garden and you're sure to attract attention. This bloom, which some call spider flower, is a top nectar source for swallowtails and hummers. Cleome's tall stems, topped by wispy pink, purple or white flowers, are hard to miss. Plants tend to reseed themselves from one year to the next if goldfinches don't get to them first!

Coral Bells

Heuchera sanguinea • Zones 3 to 8
Wands of primarily red bell-shaped flowers and handsome, sometimes evergreen foliage make this bloomer a valuable addition to any garden, whether it's located in a sunny or shady spot. This adaptable mounding plant is a striking border or container plant and will increase hummingbird traffic in your yard. To extend coral bells' blooming season, clip off spent stems.

Coreopsis

Coreopsis spp. • Zones 3 to 11
Though you can find annual varieties of this graceful plant that's easy to grow from seed, make sure you pick up one of the perennial versions, too. It loves the sun and grows well in dry conditions. A rainbow of new varieties offers striking alternatives to the traditional yellow blooms. Plants range from 8 to 48 inches in height. After the butterfly-attracting flowers fade, songbirds eat the seeds.

Cosmos

Cosmos spp. • annual
Throughout the growing season, birds and butterflies can't resist these colorful, pinwheel-shaped blossoms with feathery foliage. Grow single or double cultivars of this easygoing bloomer in full sun, and you'll have flowers and seeds from summer through late fall. Plants stand from 1 to 6 feet high, so no matter how large your space, there's a type of cosmos that will fit right in.

Crocosmia

Crocosmia spp. • Zones 5 to 9
This dramatic hummingbird magnet reaches 3 feet high, unfurling wiry stems of bright blossoms from mid- to late summer. Moist soil is important for optimal flowering. Crocosmia makes an excellent cut flower and adds tropical flair to any space, outdoors or in. But be warned: It's invasive in some areas.

Floss Flower

Globe Thistle

Flowering Tobacco

Fuchsia

Garden Phlox

Floss Flower
Ageratum houstonianum
grown as an annual
Floss flower's fuzzy clusters make soft landing pads for hungry butterflies. This fast-growing plant is common in sunny garden borders and containers thanks to its compact size: a petite 6 to 12 inches. Purple, pink, blue or white blooms are sure to beckon fliers-by.

Flowering Tobacco
Nicotiana spp. • grown as an annual
For a no-fuss way to liven up your garden, plant flowering tobacco! Ranging from 10 inches to 5 feet high, the stems are covered with star-shaped flowers in shades of red, maroon, lavender, white, pink, yellow and even green. Some types, including members of the *N. sylvestris* species, have a lovely scent, especially in the evening.

Fuchsia
Fuchsia spp. • annual to Zone 8
Fuchsia's showy, pendulous red, white, pink and purple blooms will capture your heart. There are more than 100 kinds, from low-growing dwarfs and trailing plants to upright shrubs. Fuchsia grows best in moist soil and partial shade, so it's ideal for attracting hummingbirds to less-than-sunny yards. Fertilize weekly for best results.

Garden Phlox
Phlox paniculata • Zones 3 to 8
People love the sweet fragrance of this charming classic, but butterflies and hummingbirds visit for the nectar. A tough, reliable plant, garden phlox blooms all summer with a little deadheading. Grow this pretty plant, which can reach up to 3 feet tall, in full sun, and water regularly.

Globe Thistle
Echinops ritro • Zones 3 to 9
Butterflies will be anything *but* blue when you plant this spiny-looking azure beauty in your garden. Standing up to 2 feet tall, globe thistle, also known as blue hedgehog, grows best in poor but well-draining soil and full sun. Butterflies, bees and moths relish the nectar, and once seed heads form, finches and other birds will stop by to eat.

Heliotrope
Heliotropium arborescens
grown as an annual
Heliotrope's fruity scent has earned it the nickname cherry pie. Its compact growth habit and profuse purplish blooms make it a good choice for containers and flower beds. Plants reach 2 feet tall and up to 15 inches wide. Watch yours for all types of butterflies, from blues to monarchs.

Heliotrope

Hollyhock
Alcea rosea • Zones 3 to 9
If you want to make an impact in your garden, look no further than this tall host plant to butterfly larvae, including hairstreaks, skippers and painted ladies. It comes in many colors, attracts a variety of insects and hummingbirds and can reach up to 8 feet tall. Hollyhock is a biennial, so it grows foliage on short stems its first year but doesn't flower until the next. From then on, it self-seeds.

Impatiens
Impatiens spp. • grown as an annual
Invite winged creatures into the shade with impatiens. Sparrows, finches, grosbeaks and buntings eat the seeds, while hummingbirds and butterflies drop in for a sip of nectar. Growing 6 inches to 2 feet high, impatiens has a mounding growth habit, making it a good choice for borders, foundation beds and containers.

Lantana
Lantana camara • annual to Zone 9
With its abundant clusters of tiny, nectar-rich flowers, why wouldn't hummingbirds and butterflies, including swallowtails and hairstreaks, love lantana? Later in the growing season, birds nibble its berries, as well. In more tropical climates, lantana is grown as a shrub and can become invasive. With a mounding or trailing habit, smaller varieties work well in containers.

Lavender
Lavandula spp. • Zones 5 to 10
In the summertime, hummingbirds, skippers, painted ladies and other pollinators frequently visit lavender. You'll love this Mediterranean bloomer for its attractive flower spires, silvery-green foliage and calming scent. Varieties of this flower grow from 1 to 4 feet tall, and are available in many shades of purple as well as white and light pink.

Nasturtium
Tropaeolum spp. • annual
Humans aren't the only ones who enjoy nasturtiums: Butterfly and moth caterpillars like to munch on its leaves, as do some songbirds. The nectar attracts many types of fliers. Once it's established, nasturtium performs best when left alone, contributing vivid color all season long. Some types grow in mounds, while others are good climbers.

New York Ironweed
Vernonia noveboracensis
Zones 5 to 9
Add rustic charm to your garden with New York ironweed's clouds of purple flowers, which butterflies love. Birds like the autumn seed heads. This North American native blooms in August and September on sturdy, statuesque stems. The adaptable, sun-loving perennial flourishes in any moist to normal soil.

Look at gardens across North America, and **you're likely to spot the ever-popular salvia**. We like the long-blooming Salsa series, available in single colors—from plum to white to bright red—or mixes. Want something on the tall side? Lighthouse Red reaches 18 to 24 inches.

Penstemon

Salvia

Penstemon

Penstemon spp. • Zones 3 to 10
Hummingbirds favor this spiky trumpet-shaped flower, which comes in pink, red, purple, blue and white. Varieties reach heights of up to 4 feet and bloom profusely for most or all of the summer. Full sun and well-draining soil, including the sandy stuff, are ideal.

Pentas

Pentas lanceolata • grown as an annual
Also called star clusters, these tropical beauties are a natural choice for butterfly gardens. Pentas are found in many colors, from deep red to white, and make excellent nectar plants. Grow this flower, in varieties ranging from 8 inches to 3 feet high, in full sun.

Pincushion Flower

Scabiosa spp. • Zones 4 to 9
This plant gets its name from the way its stamens stick into the flower head. Whether you choose the annual or perennial variety, 1- to 3-foot-tall pincushion flower comes in purple, maroon, white and near-black.

Red-Hot Poker

Kniphofia spp. • Zones 4 to 9
Terrific in mixed flower borders or small groupings, torchlike red-hot poker plants grow up to 4 feet high and deliver bright plumes of orange, red,

Pentas

Showy Milkweed

yellow, white and green. For best results, well-draining soil is important; the roots will rot in boggy conditions. Nectaring birds and swallowtails love it.

Salvia

Salvia splendens • grown as an annual
Also known as firecracker plant, this annual variety of salvia pops in any garden, producing season-long color in just about any landscape. Depending on the cultivar, this annual will reach 8 inches to 2 feet, though newer varieties are on the compact side.

Showy Milkweed

Asclepias speciosa • Zones 3 to 9
This 3- to 6-foot-tall butterfly magnet and monarch host boasts rose-colored flowers of 3 to 5 inches, along with silvery foliage. In the wild, it's found in Western and Central North America, growing along sandy and rocky shores and in prairies. Showy milkweed thrives in moist, well-draining soil (including rock-filled sites), but also tolerates more arid conditions.

Snapdragon

Antirrhinum majus • annual
Despite the intimidating name, butterflies (including common buckeye caterpillars) love the snapdragon. It's easily recognized by its distinctive overlapping petals, which come in appealing hues of pink, red, yellow, orange, white, purple and bronze, plus bicolors. Though it usually blooms throughout the growing season, snapdragon is most floriferous when temperatures are cooler.

Stokes' Aster

Stokesia laevis • Zones 5 to 9
Colorful fringed petals fan out from the center of this native daisy that's beloved by butterflies. Each amply sized bloom ranges from 3 to 5 inches wide, creating an impressive display in a flower bed border. Regular deadheading will extend the bloom time, sometimes even into fall.

Pincushion Flower

Snapdragon

Red-Hot Poker

Stokes' Aster

Swamp Milkweed

Sweet William

Verbena

Veronica

Yarrow

Zinnia

Swamp Milkweed
Asclepias incarnata • Zones 3 to 9
A fragrant nectar and host plant, swamp milkweed is a top performer in moist soil. Less pushy than common milkweed, this 3- to 5-foot native blooms in white or pink.

Sweet William
Dianthus barbatus • Zones 3 to 9
A biennial beauty, sweet William tends to grow to about 2 feet tall, but dwarf varieties are easy to come by, as well. Each flower-packed stem makes a complete bouquet!

Verbena
Verbena x *hybrida* • annual to Zone 9
Expect summerlong color from these attractive blooms. The plant's stems spread out to about 18 inches. Keep the soil moist but well drained for optimal flowering.

Veronica
Veronica spp. • Zones 3 to 9
Ever-popular veronica has a wide range of growing habits, and blooms in cool shades. It thrives in well-draining, fertile soil and full sun, but tolerates part shade.

Yarrow
Achillea spp. • Zones 3 to 9
This easygoing, long-lasting perennial ranges from 6 inches to nearly 5 feet high. Yarrow comes in a rainbow of colors and is suited to most growing conditions.

Zinnia
Zinnia spp. • annual
A hummingbird and butterfly garden go-to, several varieties of sparrows, finches and juncos eat seeds later in the year. It reaches up to 3 feet and blooms until the first frost.

shrubs & trees

Abelia
Abelia spp. • Zones 6 to 11
When abelia's sweet, trumpet-shaped flowers open, you'll know that spring is in full swing. Cue the hummingbirds and butterflies! Varieties of this long-blooming shrub reach between 5 and 15 feet tall, growing best in a sunny spot protected from the wind.

Blue Spirea
Caryopteris spp. • Zones 5 to 9
Add some cool hues to your landscape, and you'll be seeing butterflies in no time. Blue spirea's tiers of blue or purple florets make this a late-summer all-star. Most types of this shrub are about 3-1/2 feet tall and 5 feet wide and grow best in light, well-draining soil in full sun or light shade.

Butterfly Bush
Buddleja davidii • Zones 5 to 9
A top nectar plant for many winged species, heat- and drought-tolerant butterfly bush grows up to 15 feet tall. The arching branches are tipped with tiny purple, white, pink or yellow blooms from midsummer through frost. It's invasive in some areas.

Buttonbush
Cephalanthus occidentalis
Zones 5 to 10
Round white flower heads with needlelike protrusions make honey-sweet buttonbush unmistakable. Shrubs are generally about 6 feet tall but occasionally far surpass that. Consistently moist soil is a must; downright wet soil, a plus.

Fringe Tree
Chionanthus virginicus • Zones 3 to 9
The fringe tree entices butterflies with its panicles of creamy-white flowers. This slow-growing tall shrub or tree usually starts from seed and tends to reach just 20 feet. Sphinx moths use the fringe tree as a host plant, and more than 75 species of birds are known to feast on its blue-black fruit.

Hibiscus
Hibiscus spp. • Zones 5 to 11
Bold, beautiful and impressive, this exotic-looking shrub grows up to 15 feet tall. Its flowers alone span up to 12 inches wide, beckoning fliers of all types, and last from early summer till the first frost. Plant this stunner in rich, moist soil in a sunny site.

Don't assume the worst if your **fringe tree seems particularly slow to leaf out**. It unfurls its strappy flowers first, but not till the onset of summer.

Abelia

Butterfly Bush

Fringe Tree

Blue Spirea

Buttonbush

Hibiscus

Potentilla

Potentilla fruticosa • Zones 2 to 7
When many other flowering shrubs'
show is all but a memory, potentilla,
or bush cinquefoil, is just beginning its
long blooming season. The pink, yellow,
red or white blossoms of this drought-
tolerant plant will last until the first hard
frost, attracting migrating butterflies. Its
dense branches provide protection for
birds year-round. This compact shrub is
about 3 feet high and up to 5 feet wide.

Serviceberry

Amelanchier spp. • Zones 2 to 9
Looking for a birds-and-blooms bonanza
for your yard? Try serviceberry. These
small trees or shrubs, which thrive in
sun or part shade, provide many months
of interest, with butterfly-friendly spring
flowers, summer berries that songbirds
enjoy, plus colorful fall foliage.

Summersweet

Clethra alnifolia • Zones 3 to 9
Native to the Eastern U.S., fragrant
summersweet is a pretty addition to
any shady site. Spikes bearing bell-
shaped pink or white blooms emerge
in late summer, just in time to entice
southbound fliers. Summersweet
reaches 8 feet tall; for a smaller space,
try Hummingbird—it's 2 to 3 feet tall.

Yucca

Yucca filamentosa • Zones 4 to 11
There's a good reason that so many
gardeners (especially those in the
Southwest) use yucca as a backyard
centerpiece. It's about as drought-
tolerant as they come. Spiky evergreen
leaves create a mound that's so
substantial that birds nest within it,
while hummingbirds crave the nectar
the beautiful columnar white flowers
provide. Types of this shrub can reach
3 to 12 feet tall when in bloom.

vines

Passionflower

Passiflora spp. • Zones 7 to 9
This quirky flower doesn't just look cool,
it's a big draw for Southern wildlife.
Nectar-seekers visit blossoms, while
certain types of longwings and other
butterflies use the vine as a host. The
fragrant flowers come in shades of
purple, blue, red, pink, yellow and white,
and make way for berries that birds
devour. Vines range in length from 15 to
50 feet—most gardeners let the tendrils
climb walls and fences, while others use
it as a groundcover.

Trumpet Honeysuckle

Lonicera sempervirens • Zones 4 to 9
Plant this and you won't be the only
one to fall for its elegant blossoms:
Hummingbirds are suckers for trumpet
honeysuckle, too. Vines with red, orange
and yellow blossoms climb up to 20 feet
and thrive in full sun to partial shade.
Once the blooms fade, finches, thrushes
and other songbirds will stop by to
nibble the berries. This North American
native is also host to the spring azure
and the snowberry clearwing moth.

Trumpet Vine

Campsis radicans • Zones 4 to 9
There's a reason you see so many
photos of hummingbirds at trumpet vine.
They love this sweet beauty! A perennial
classic, trumpet vine grows up to 40
feet, easily filling a trellis with its orange-
red or yellow blooms. The trumpet vine
sphinx moth uses it as a host plant.
Unwanted suckers will generally be
discouraged if cut off.

Help stop trumpet
vine—which has a penchant
for spreading—from invading your
garden and lawn. **Plant it in a large,
sturdy container.** Prune and deadhead
regularly to keep it in check.

Potentilla

Yucca

Serviceberry

Passionflower

Summersweet

Trumpet Honeysuckle

Trumpet Vine

double duty

When you're hungry, there's nothing like freshly harvested produce—and birds and butterflies agree. Here are 10 favorites we share.

Apple
Malus spp. • Zones 3 to 8
The apple is cultivated across North America for its pretty spring flowers and tasty late-season fruit. It's a host to the white admiral. Grosbeaks nibble the flower buds and robins, thrushes and others flock for the fruit. It prefers moist but well-draining soil and full sun.

Blueberry
Vaccinium spp. • Zones 3 to 10
Producing bell-shaped white flowers in spring and plump, flavorful fruits in summer, this shrub supplies food for butterflies, birds, small mammals and humans. The blueberry is a plant for all seasons: Green leaves turn to orange or red in autumn, and the bright stems are attractive through winter.

Broccoli
Brassica oleracea italica • annual
A host plant for cabbage white butterfly larvae, broccoli also attracts the birds that feed on the caterpillars. This member of the cabbage family is ready to eat about two months after planting.

Carrot
Daucus carota var. *sativus* • annual
It's not the crunchy orange spikes that entice black swallowtail caterpillars, it's the tops. Plant the tiny seeds in loose, well-draining soil for best results—and if you want long, straight carrots, be sure the soil is rock-free, too.

Dill
Anethum graveolens • annual
Don't be surprised if you see eastern black swallowtails flitting among dill's green fronds: This herb is a larval host plant. In summer and fall, yellow blooms open on broad flower heads. At 3 to 4 feet tall, dill sometimes needs to be staked. It thrives in well-draining, sandy or loamy soil.

Fennel
Foeniculum vulgare • annual
With a dill-like top and stems that resemble celery, you could assume fennel tastes like a cross between the two. Nope! Instead, think licorice. Attractive to butterflies and other beneficial insects, as well as songbirds, fennel reaches about 3 feet tall and prefers rich, well-draining soil.

Parsley
Petroselinum crispum • tender biennial
It's a must for herb gardens and butterfly gardens, too, since parsley is a host plant for the eastern black swallowtail. With curly or flat leaves, it prefers cooler temps and grows best in full sun and slightly acidic soil.

Pear
Pyrus communis • Zones 5 to 9
A pear tree is a pretty and practical addition to a wildlife garden. Reaching up to 50 feet tall, this tree has lovely spring blooms and autumn foliage. Many types of butterflies—anglewings, hackberries and admirals—and birds enjoy the fruit.

Scarlet Runner Bean
Phaseolus coccineus • annual to Zone 7
Scarlet flowers on 20-foot vines attract both hummingbirds and butterflies. You can eat the purple-and-black beans right off the vine—delicious!—or cook them. Keep the plant looking tidy with a trellis, arbor, fence or tepee.

Strawberry
Fragaria spp. • Zones 2 to 11
This sweet treat will bring lots of fliers to your yard. Plants have various growing habits, so choose the one that's right for you. Just remember that you won't be able to harvest the fruit until the second growing season. The wait will be worth it!

Apple

Fennel

Blueberry

Parsley

Broccoli

Pear

Carrot

Scarlet Runner Bean

Dill

Strawberry

WARM-WEATHER *gardens*
FOR BIRDS & BUTTERFLIES

Heat up summer with these wildlife magnets.

Give your favorite winged creatures lots of reasons to call your yard home this summer. Want to make these garden plans even more attractive? Include a birdbath or a feeder in the design!

Warm Welcome

Greet guests and nearby fliers with a cheery combination of summer bloomers planted around your lamppost.

1. **Trumpet honeysuckle** *Lonicera sempervirens*, Zones 4 to 9

2. **Rose** *Rosa* spp., Zones 2 to 9

3. **Lavender** *Lavandula* spp., Zones 5 to 10

4. **Nasturtium** *Tropaeolum majus*, annual

5. **Sweet alyssum** *Lobularia maritima*, annual

When selecting a rosebush for your bird-and-butterfly paradise, choices abound. The key is to **pick a type that's fragrant and produces nectar**, so old-fashioned roses are a good bet. You can further increase traffic and extend the garden's appeal by letting rose hips form: No deadheading allowed!

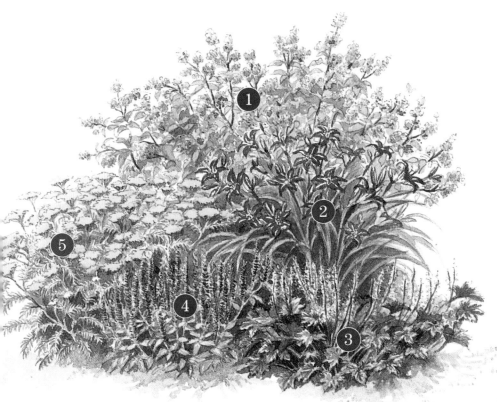

Primary Pleasures

A sunny spot is the ideal locale for this group. The light enhances color, encourages blooming and strengthens the plants' structure.

1. **California lilac** *Ceanothus* x *delilianus* 'Gloire de Versailles,' Zones 7 to 11
2. **Daylily** *Hemerocallis* spp., Zones 3 to 10
3. **Coral bells** *Heuchera* spp., Zones 3 to 9
4. **Meadow sage** *Salvia nemorosa*, Zones 5 to 9
5. **Yarrow** *Achillea* 'Moonshine,' Zones 3 to 9

Blossoming Buffet

Including a variety of shapes, sizes and shades is a smart way to maximize traffic to your wildlife garden—this way, you offer something for everyone.

1. **Butterfly bush** *Buddleja davidii*, Zones 5 to 9
2. **Globe thistle** *Echinops ritro*, Zones 3 to 9
3. **Penstemon** *Penstemon* spp., Zones 3 to 10
4. **Catmint** *Nepeta* x *faassenii*, Zones 3 to 8
5. **Osteospermum** *Osteospermum* spp., annual

 Turn the page to take your butterfly garden design one step further!

GARDEN FOR
butterflies

Invite butterflies to your backyard with a specially designed garden filled with their favorite eats.

Total size: 10 × 10 feet

GARDEN PLANS AND DIRECTIONS: SALLY ROTH; BUTTERFLY ILLUSTRATIONS: MELISSA SWEET; SWALLOWTAIL: ANGELA HARDY

Perfect Pairings
This vibrant plan of perennials and annuals (above) partners host plants and nectar plants.

1. **Dwarf butterfly bush** *Buddleja davidii*, Zones 5 to 9 ~ 2 plants

2. **Coneflower** *Echinacea* spp., Zones 3 to 9 ~ 2 plants

3. **Purpletop vervain** *Verbena bonariensis*, annual to Zone 7 ~ 2 plants

4. **Autumn Joy sedum** *Sedum* spp., Zones 3 to 9 ~ 6 plants

5. **Bronze fennel** *Foeniculum vulgare*, grown as an annual ~ 2 plants

6. **Mönch aster** *Aster* x *frikartii* 'Mönch,' Zones 5 to 8 ~ 2 plants

7. **Broccoli** *Brassica oleracea italica*, grown as an annual ~ 6 plants

8. **Oregano** *Origanum vulgare*, Zones 4 to 9 ~ 2 plants

9. **Anise hyssop** *Agastache foeniculum*, Zones 4 to 11 ~ 3 plants

10. **Pinkish-purple swamp milkweed** *Asclepias incarnata*, Zones 3 to 9 ~ 2 plants

11. **Purple annual verbena** *Verbena* spp., annual ~ 6 plants

12. **Lantana** *Lantana camara*, annual to Zone 8 ~ 2 plants

13. **Floss flower** *Ageratum houstonianum*, grown as an annual ~ 6 plants

14. **White sweet alyssum** *Lobularia maritima*, annual ~ about 12 plants

15. **Persian Carpet zinnia** *Zinnia haageana* 'Persian Carpet,' annual ~ about 12 plants

Nectar Feast

These amazing annuals (below) will be the new dining digs for local butterflies in no time.

1. **Floss flower** *Ageratum houstonianum*, grown as an annual ~ 12 to 14 plants
2. **Purple annual verbena** *Verbena* spp., annual ~ 2 plants
3. **Red annual verbena** *Verbena* spp., annual ~ 2 to 4 plants
4. **Purple sweet alyssum** *Lobularia maritima*, annual ~ about 12 plants
5. **White sweet alyssum** *Lobularia maritima*, annual ~ about 20 plants
6. **Parsley** *Petroselinum* spp., tender biennial ~ 4 plants
7. **Bronze fennel** *Foeniculum vulgare*, grown as an annual ~ 2 plants
8. **Low-growing zinnias** *Zinnia* spp., annual ~ 2 to 4 seed packets
9. **Lemon Gem marigolds** *Tagetes* 'Lemon Gem,' annual ~ 4 to 6 seed packets
10. **Tangerine Gem marigolds** *Tagetes* 'Tangerine Gem,' annual ~ 2 seed packets

building your butterfly bed

Use these simple steps to create exactly the shape of garden you want.

1. A place of honor in your lawn, in full sun, is perfect for your butterfly garden. To fully appreciate the effect, **find a site that gives you a view from above**, too.

2. Measure a 10- by 10-foot square or an 18- by 10-foot rectangle. Use stakes to mark the corners and **tie on twine to outline the garden.**

3. Use white flour to draw the butterfly shape. For a guideline to wing placement, divide the area into quarters by sprinkling out two intersecting lines, one vertical and one horizontal. Then draw one wing in each quarter.

4. Remove lawn grass: Slice a line 4 to 5 inches deep along the butterfly with an edger or spade. Then use a sharp, flat shovel or a sod cutter to slice through roots. Roll up the sod like a carpet.

5. Turn soil with a spade, breaking up clods, and rake it smooth. **Add several inches of organic matter** to improve soil.

6. Edge your butterfly with a mowing strip to keep the lines clean and make lawn mowing easy.

7. Set the transplant pots in place, and then **plant each one.** Finally, sow seeds for the fast-growing annuals, according to whichever garden design you choose.

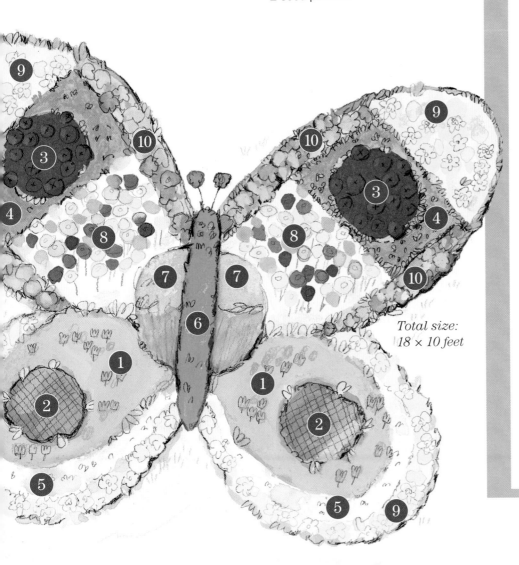

Total size: 18 × 10 feet

SIZZLING SUMMER
containers

Create hot spots for birds and butterflies with these flower-filled containers.

Ⓑ

Ⓐ

Sunsational

Combine heat and sun lovers like these for a carefree, cheerful mix that will bloom long into fall.

LIGHT REQUIREMENT: Sun

POT SIZE: 16 inches

INGREDIENTS:

A. Superbells® Peach calibrachoa
3 plants

B. Tuscan Sun perennial sunflower
2 plants

Ⓑ

Ⓐ Ⓑ Ⓐ

Ⓐ

Towering Treasures

Make a big statement with a tall combo bursting with blooms.

LIGHT REQUIREMENT: Sun

POT SIZE: 24 inches

INGREDIENTS:

A. Variegatus dwarf white-striped sweet flag ~ 2 plants

B. Angelface® White angelonia ~ 2 plants

C. Licorice Splash licorice plant ~ 1 plant

D. Atlantis heliotrope ~ 1 plant

E. Laguna™ Compact Blue with Eye lobelia ~ 3 plants

F. Icterina golden leaf sage ~ 1 plant

Blues Quartet

Plant a veritable buffet for butterflies by choosing blooms in the most tempting shades.

LIGHT REQUIREMENT: Sun

POT SIZE: 30 inches

INGREDIENTS:

A. Artist® Blue floss flower ~ 3 plants

B. Superbells® Blue calibrachoa ~ 3 plants

C. Snowstorm® Blue bacopa ~ 3 plants

D. Superbena® Large Lilac Blue verbena
3 plants

Sweet Nectar

Get loads of backyard buzz all season by including this vibrant combo in your landscape.

LIGHT REQUIREMENT: Sun

POT SIZE: 14 inches

INGREDIENTS:

A. Superbells® Tequila Sunrise calibrachoa ~ 2 plants

B. Supertunia® Red petunia ~ 2 plants

C. Luscious® Citrus Blend™ lantana ~ 2 plants

Soft-Spoken

Floss flower puffballs and ruffled wishbone flower give this arrangement a soft look. Position the wishbone flower on the shadiest side.

LIGHT REQUIREMENTS: Part to full sun

POT SIZE: 14 inches

INGREDIENTS:

A. Artist® Alto Blue floss flower ~ 1 plant

B. Intensia® Neon Pink phlox ~ 1 plant

C. Catalina® Purple wishbone flower ~ 1 plant

Elegant Ice

This cool-hued blend will certainly beckon nectar-seeking fliers, from hummers to butterflies to bees.

LIGHT REQUIREMENTS: Part to full sun

POT SIZE: 36 inches

INGREDIENTS:

A. Blue Satin® rose of Sharon ~ 1 plant

B. Diamond Frost® euphorbia ~ 2 plants

C. Laguna™ Sky Blue lobelia ~ 4 plants

Rose of Sharon is part of **the hibiscus family**. The blooms lend gardens exotic flair from late summer till mid-fall.

our readers share

Where do you display containers and hanging baskets in your yard?

"I put containers on the front porch, because nothing says 'welcome' like a colorful display of flowers. I also put containers and hanging baskets around my feeders in the backyard to attract my favorite birds, such as American goldfinches and ruby-throated hummingbirds."

—RACHEL B., *Oswego, IL*

"I have containers on the deck, the porch and among perennials in the garden."

—LIZ S., *Richmond, IN*

"We hang them in bird-friendly areas: tree limbs, quiet sunny areas on the porch, shepherd's hooks in the flower and veggie gardens and the barn eaves. We have many finches and low-nesting birds, and they love our flower containers."

—SUSAN P., *via Facebook*

"I hang baskets everywhere: under oak and cherry trees, on the porch and on my fence. Where the sun is, I will plant!" —CHRISTA A., *Monterey, CA*

"I live in a townhouse, so I have limited space. I hang baskets from shepherd's hooks, which I reuse in winter to hold suet baskets, bird feeders, etc."

—KIM S., *via Facebook*

"Mine is in front of the kitchen window so I can see it while washing the dishes." —JACK M., *Brockport, PA*

"We put them under our pergola. In Colorado, the sun is so strong and the humidity so low that the annuals dry up and fry in the middle of summer. Our flowers need a little sun protection."

—SARA R., *via Facebook*

summer BIRDING basics

WHO'S THERE?
Look for these birds in your yard.

MOURNING DOVE ANTICS: These gentle birds with the mournful song are some of the most entertaining nesters around. You can find them throughout North America building unkempt nests out of sticks and twigs. These sloppy nests don't always hold together well, but mourning doves can afford to lose an egg now and then: They have four or five broods each nesting season.

HUMMINGBIRD HEAVEN: By June all your hummers have arrived and are nesting. Sometimes feeder activity will drop in June and early July, because mama hummingbirds are feeding their babies live insects. But don't give up. Activity will increase later as new families discover your feeders.

FLEDGLING FUN: By the time young birds leave the nest they're almost as big as their parents, so look for these clues to know you're seeing a fledgling. Youngsters often flap their wings while loudly begging their parents for food. They may have a rumpled look—as if they're having a bad hair day.

WHAT'S ON THE MENU?
What to feed your summer visitors.

A WRIGGLY BUFFET: Lots of birds love mealworms—just ask my coworker Nelson Ferguson, who feeds his backyard bluebirds every summer morning. The adults wait patiently for him to set the worms in a bowl by their house; then they deliver the soft, easy-to-eat worms to their hungry babies. Before long, the whole family is coming for breakfast.

NO-MESS BIRDSEED: Bird feeding can be messy. Discarded shells and sprouting seeds don't do a lot to enhance your outdoor relaxing or entertaining. Often called "no-mess blend" or "sunflower chip," this hull-less option is more expensive but worth the extra cost if tidy dining is your goal.

HOOKED ON HUMANS? If you're going on vacation, don't worry about where your feathered friends

Both bluebird parents **share the responsibilities** of raising nestlings and fledglings.

You'll see plenty of activity at feeders and birdbaths in the summer. BY ANNE SCHMAUSS

CEDAR WAXWING: MICHAEL R. DUNCAN; ROBIN: GLORIA ANDRES; BLUEBIRDS: MICHEATWOOD

will find food. Birds don't become dependent upon you. They'll learn to fend for themselves no matter how much food you provide. What you offer is only a fraction of their diet. Most of their food comes from natural sources, which are especially abundant during the summer months.

IN A NUTSHELL
Don't miss these just-in-time tips!

MORE ROOM AT THE TABLE: Consider adding another seed feeder. As your bird population increases, competition at the feeder can be fierce. My favorite extra feeder is a ground tray with legs. Place it anywhere in your yard to offer plenty of space for large and small birds alike. Use a mix of sunflower and millet in your ground tray.

COOL, COOL WATER: A birdbath can help hot birds get cool. Bathing is often vigorous in warmer months: You've probably seen a robin family splash all the water out of your bath in minutes. It's also fun to watch awkward fledglings try to figure out

how to use your bath. As usual, your birdbath is often the best place to spot birds that don't eat seed, including warblers, tanagers and vireos.

BIRD FOOD NATURALLY: Birds harvest seeds from blooms like sunflowers, coneflowers and cosmos. Fruiting trees and shrubs such as hawthorn, Virginia creeper and mountain ash feed a wide variety of birds, including robins, cedar waxwings, catbirds and mockingbirds. Honeysuckle, trumpet vine, impatiens and some other flowers provide high-energy nectar for hummers.

FIRST, DO NO HARM: If you see a young bird on the ground that has its feathers and is able to hop around, don't assume it's been abandoned. In most cases, the bird doesn't need help, and by trying to rescue it we may be doing more harm than good. When young birds leave the nest, their parents continue to care for them until they learn to fly and fend for themselves. Do keep pets and kids away from these fledglings until they're strong fliers.

BUSY BACKYARD.
By nurturing a wildlife garden, you're sure to see a wide variety of birds each summer, including mourning doves (far left), hummingbirds (left), American goldfinches (center), cedar waxwings (far right), American robins (above) and eastern bluebirds (top).

Common Buckeye

YEAR-ROUND
butterflies:
SUMMER

This time of year, flying jewels are everywhere. BY KENN KAUFMAN

From the fringes of the tropics to the Arctic, summer is high season for North American butterflies.

Learning the Life Cycle

A large and diverse garden may be alive with butterflies all summer long. If we watch casually, it might seem that we're seeing the same ones throughout the season, but the reality is more complicated and more interesting than that.

Most adult butterflies live only two or three weeks at most. With common small butterflies like pearl crescents or tailed blues, the first females to emerge in spring or early summer will lay eggs that will soon hatch. The caterpillars will grow rapidly and pupate, and another batch of adults will appear; there may be three or more generations during the warmer months. Populations of these species may seem to rise and fall.

Shorter summers often mean fewer generations. Several kinds of butterflies, such as some of the swallowtails, may have several broods per year in the Deep South, but only one in the North. And some have a single generation each year regardless of latitude, including the great spangled fritillary.

Regional Standouts

In Arctic Canada and Alaska, a few butterflies—mostly lesser fritillaries and satyrs—fly every other year. Summers are so short that the caterpillars hatch in one season, hibernate through one winter, feed and grow through the following summer, then hibernate through a second winter before pupating and emerging as adults in their second summer. Some observers may be puzzled to find that a species could be common one summer and seemingly absent the next.

At the opposite climate extreme, summer is the time when southern butterflies push northward. Tropical sulphurs and skippers may move north from Mexico into the American Southwest; widespread butterflies like buckeyes and red admirals may move north past the Great Lakes. By summer's end, migratory monarchs have reached northern regions, far into Canada, poised for the seasonal change that will send them drifting south.

GLAD YOU ASKED

Make your backyard a wildlife wonderland with these summer solutions from our experts.

CHASING FIREFLIES

I'd like to **attract fireflies to my yard**. Are there any plants that entice them?

—ANNE H., *Fort Madison, IA*

MELINDA MYERS: A change in gardening habits will help bring in the fireflies. Try growing the grass long. The adults lay their eggs in the soil; the larvae feed on snails, slugs and worms. Eliminate the use of chemicals to preserve their food source. Also, limit outdoor lighting that can interfere with their light signals: Too much light and they don't glow. Include low-hanging trees and other vegetation that will provide daytime perches for these insects.

VINE WON'T CLIMB

I planted **hummingbird vine** 2 years ago, but it will not grow. The vine won't even try to climb the fence that's next to it. Can you please give me some advice?

—THOMAS L., *Constantine, MI*

MELINDA: Several plants go by the name hummingbird vine. The large orange and yellow flowered trumpet vine (*Campsis radicans*) attaches to structures with its aerial roots.

The bright-orange, coral-red or scarlet blooming honeysuckle vine (*Lonicera* spp., shown here) also attracts hummingbirds. It attaches itself to structures by twining around the support.

Once you know which variety you have, make sure you give it the support it needs. A brick wall is a good choice for trumpet vine, while a trellis or arbor is more suitable for the honeysuckle.

You may need to provide a bit of training and guidance in the beginning. Secure branches to the structure with twine or staking tape. Once the vine makes contact, it should continue to grow and cling to the structure on its own.

Proper growing conditions and care should get your vine off and growing. Trumpet vine prefers full sun and well-draining soil. Avoid types of fertilization that encourage lots of leaves and no flowers. Honeysuckle vines, on the other hand, like full sun to part shade.

 Find more expert info on the next page.

SHUTTERSTOCK.COM; FLOWER: RDA-GID

This **speckled bird** (left) sat in our mulberry tree all summer long. It has migrated for several years, each time returning to this tree. What bird is it?

—DEBRA J., *Moody, TX*

GEORGE HARRISON: This bird is a common nighthawk, which *is* common, but not a hawk. It is a member of the nightjar family, which includes whip-poor-wills, common poorwills and chuck-will's-widows.

RUB-A-DUB-DUB

My daughter and I were out taking photos of wildflowers and butterflies when **we came upon this unusual flier** (above). It would rub its wings together, so that at first glance it looked like two butterflies. What is it?

—DONNA R., *Creola, AL*

TOM ALLEN: This is the great purple hairstreak. There must have been mistletoe nearby. It's the host plant for this butterfly.

Hairstreaks are unique butterflies. If you take a close look, you'll see that these beauties rub the rear portion of their wings together a lot more than the front parts. By rubbing their rear wings together, they attract attention to the rear of their bodies. They have two—and sometimes four—small, feather-like tails on their rear wings, which look like antennae to a predator. Hairstreaks often have bright-red, orange or blue spots at the rear as well, which resemble eyes.

A bird trying to catch this butterfly will typically attack the moving rear, mistaking it for the head. Even if the bird takes a snip out of the wings, the butterfly is able to escape, virtually unharmed.

BLOOMING ATTRACTIONS

Two of my favorite butterflies are the eastern tiger swallowtail and zebra longwing, but **I can't seem to attract them to my yard.**

I keep thinking, if I plant it, they will come. But I have tulip trees, willow trees and passionvines, and still no butterflies. Can you offer more tips?

—AUSTIN M., *Sugar Land, TX*

TOM: Tiger swallowtails will only visit your yard if they are common in the area. You are near the edge of their range, but if you see them nearby, you should be able to attract them.

Planting plenty of nectar plants will catch the eye of strays. In particular, try cottonwood, sweet bay and cherry. For zebra longwings, keep using native passionvines, as they will work the best. These butterflies prefer shaded habitat, so try growing this vine up a tree. Good luck. I hope your persistence pays off!

WELCOME OWLS

Is there a way to **attract owls to the yard?** I often hear one calling behind our neighbors' house, and I'd love for it to visit our yard. —ETHAN K., *Newton Falls, OH*

GEORGE: The only action you can take to attract owls to your yard is to put up a wood duck house on a tree trunk, 20 to 30 feet above the ground. Eastern screech-owls commonly roost and nest in these houses.

I often see a screech-owl sitting in the entrance to my wood duck house at dusk. Screech-owls are found in two color phases, red and gray (Laurie Lukanich of Grapevine, Texas, sent in a great example). The color has nothing to do with their sex. You should have both types in Ohio, so perhaps you can coax one to your yard.

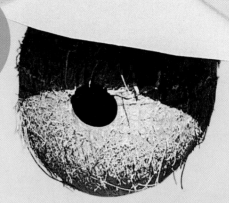

Ted has observed at least **15 broods of wrens** grow up in this coconut abode!

^ BEACH RETREAT "I built this birdhouse to help raise money for Habitat for Humanity," says Peter Moehrle of Orlando, Florida. "I designed it to resemble a traditional Malaysian home. I hope it's a popular bird retreat in someone's yard."

BACKYARD BUILDERS

Commemorate summer by displaying a beachy birdhouse like one of these in your backyard.

^ TROPICAL FLAVOR "I crafted this birdhouse by hollowing out a $1 coconut and topping it with a cone-shaped roof made from a circular piece of aluminum," writes Ted Logan of Cincinnati, Ohio. "It's not only economical, but extremely durable and easy to create."

< LIGHT UP THE NIGHT "When I build birdhouses, I like including a solar light so I can enjoy it at night," writes Eugene, Oregon, reader Robert Boyce. "Here's a lighthouse design that I made, and the birds love it. I have no problem getting 'renters.' In fact, most are inhabited two to three times a year!"

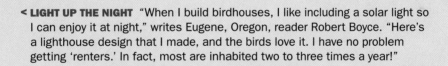

< COASTAL CREATION "We live on the coast, so we have an endless supply of shells," Linda Pollard of Hampstead, North Carolina, explains. To achieve this look, gather seashells from the beach (or buy them at a craft store) and glue them to the wood of a birdhouse using a liquid adhesive (like Liquid Nails). "The houses have been a big hit with my family and friends," she says.

< ISLAND GETAWAY "I made this Polynesian-themed birdhouse from scraps of lumber and other recycled items," Beret Dickinson of Escondido, California, tells *Birds & Blooms*. "I used a straw broom for the roof, and the perch on the top is a table leg. Now it's ready for a spot on an island."

SUMMER PROJECTS

When you're selecting supplies for the bat house, keep these hints in mind: Avoid using pressure-treated wood. Also, **choose a dark paint color to absorb heat** or maintain a more natural look with a dark shade of stain.

let's go BATTY

Insect-eating predators play a valuable role in maintaining a healthy backyard.

PROJECT AND PHOTOS BY
KRIS WETHERBEE

Nix bugs the natural way: Invite bats to stay in your backyard.

BATS GET NO RESPECT. Thanks to misconceptions perpetuated by old legends, scary stories and vampire movies, most of us think of bats as harmful or even evil creatures of the night.

Truth be told, bats are not blind, nor will they get tangled in your hair if you're outside after dark. They are not rodents, and very rarely do they transmit diseases to other animals or humans. Despite their creepy reputation, these furry, warm-blooded creatures are gentle, quiet and shy. And best of all, bats eat lots of insects, so you can spend more time enjoying summer's gorgeous weather!

By adding a bat house to your backyard, you can attract interesting wildlife while decreasing pesky bugs. Ready to build a bat house? Let's get started!

a

b

c

d

1. Cut plywood pieces to the sizes listed. Place the top edge of the netting 2 inches below the top of the back board. Make sure the netting is flat, then staple along the top, bottom and sides (**fig. a**).

2. To make the roof slant forward, cut off the top of each side piece so it measures 30 inches long in back and 28 inches long in front (**fig. b**).

3. Use wood glue and then screws to assemble. First, attach the side pieces to the back so that the longer, 30-inch side is 2 inches below the top of the back pieces and faces the netting. The extra length at the bottom will serve as a landing pad.

Secure the 24 x 22-inch top front piece to the front surface of the sides, keeping the two flush (**fig. c**). The top piece should be attached 4 inches below the tops of the back pieces.

Attach the lower 24 x 6-inch front piece to the sides, leaving a 1/2-inch ventilation gap between it and the upper front piece. This piece should be 3-1/2 inches above the bottom of the back.

4. Attach the 2-inch side of the entry guard board to the back. Make sure the top edge is flush with the bottom edges of the side pieces and secure. (This will make the opening to the chamber about 1 inch, allowing bats to enter but keeping predators out.) Attach the top piece to the sides and secure.

5. To attach the optional metal roof, use screws to secure the metal piece to the top. Here's where you can be creative. If you don't want to use the metal decorative piece, try something else to dress it up.

Caulk around the outside of the roof and sides, if needed, to seal the roosting chamber. Next, apply primer to the wood surfaces, if desired, and then stain or paint all wood surfaces at least twice in whatever color you desire.

6. It's time to start attracting these great fliers to your backyard! Attach your bat house to a post, a tree or along the outside of a building in a sunny spot (**fig. d**), at least 12 feet above the ground so bats can easily fly in and out.

WHAT YOU NEED

Safety glasses

Saw

One 3 x 4-foot piece of exterior plywood, cut into these pieces:
- 24 x 36-inch (back)
- 24 x 22-inch (top front)
- 24 x 6-inch (lower front)
- 24 x 4-inch (top roof)

One 24 x 34-inch piece of 1/8-inch-thick plastic mesh, netting or shade cloth

Stapler

Tape measure

Two 2 x 2 x 30-inch pieces of pine or cedar (sides)

Wood glue

Wood clamps

Electric drill

20 to 30 1-inch screws

5 to 10 1-1/2-inch screws

One 1 x 2 x 24-inch piece of pine or cedar (entry guard)

One 24 x 4-inch piece of metal flashing (roof, optional)

Caulking gun (optional)

1 tube paintable acrylic caulk (optional)

Paintbrushes

1 pint water-based exterior primer (optional)

1 quart flat water-based exterior paint or stain

Jazz
up a small
space with this
**charming little
feeder**. Or create
a big impact by
hanging several
in a row.

FEEDER
in a jar

**Turn a recycled baby food jar into a pretty, practical
sugar-water hummingbird feeder.** BY KRIS DRAKE

HUMMINGBIRDS ARE EASY TO PLEASE. They don't require a fancy
feeder or a special mixture. This sugar-water feeder cost nearly
nothing to make. It's a fun project you can finish in just a few hours,
and it's ideal for kids, too. Good luck attracting hummingbirds!

WHAT YOU NEED

Clean, shallow jar with lid

Rolling pin

Polymer clay (including
red, hummers' favorite)

Flower-shaped cookie
cutters (optional)

Oven

Drill

32-inch piece of 16-
gauge galvanized wire

Wire cutters

Needle-nose pliers

Glass beads

Sugar water

1. Use a rolling pin to
flatten the clay. Take the
color you want to be the
flower base and press it
onto the top of the jar lid
to remove any air pockets.
Then trim off any excess
and smooth clay down the
sides of the lid.

2. Using the other clay
colors, design the flower to
rest on this base. Roll out
the clay and experiment
with different shapes
and designs. Use cookie
cutters, or just freestyle it.

3. After you've cut out the
clay, start layering. This
gives the illusion of a real
flower, which will bring in
the hummingbirds!

4. Gently press the layers
of clay onto the lid base.
Pushing too hard may
smudge your design, but
you do want the layers to
fuse when you bake them.

5. Bake according to the
directions on the clay you
are using. A pretty good
approximation is to bake at
275° for 15 minutes.

6. Allow the clay to cool;
then drill a small hole
through the top of the clay
flower lid. This will give the
hummingbirds access to
the nectar.

7. Fold wire in half, leaving
a loop at the top. Make a
larger loop with each end
of the wire, then twist them
together about eight times.
Bend the loops to find a
design you like. Wrap each
end of the wire around the
jar, bringing them together
and twisting three times,
making a tight loop to
secure the feeder.

8. Trim the excess wire,
leaving 1/4-inch for a loop
to add beads. Fill with
nectar and enjoy!

pint-sized POND

All you need is a barrel to create a tiny pool of serenity that provides water for birds.

MOST OF US WOULD LOVE TO HAVE A SOOTHING POND right outside the back door. But ponds can be expensive and time-consuming to install. And many yards simply can't accommodate the space. Don't let that stop you! This design, inspired by Christine Davis of Platte City, Missouri, is remarkably simple—that's Christine in the photos.

Submerged and floating plants are the best choices for a pond this size. The leaves of submerged plants sit at least partially below the water level. These plants act as filters, keeping the water clear and oxygenated. Floating-leaved plants, such as water lilies, shade the water, discouraging algae growth.

In just a few short hours, you—and your feathered friends—could be enjoying a refreshing tropical paradise in your own backyard.

WHAT YOU NEED

Half of a wooden barrel (available at hardware stores and garden centers)

10-foot sheet of heavy-duty plastic or preformed plastic liner

Scissors

Staple gun

1/2-inch staples

Garden hose

Water conditioner (optional)

Water plants

Cinder blocks, bricks or plastic pots

1. Select a location. A place that receives full sun and is away from debris-dropping trees is ideal. Build the pond in that spot.

2. Make sure there are no sharp objects on the interior walls of the barrel. Fold the plastic in half, center it and smooth it inside the barrel.

3. Begin filling the barrel with water, smoothing the plastic as the water rises (**fig. a**). When it's half full, stop the flow and trim the plastic at the rim, leaving an inch or two of excess.

4. Fold the excess plastic toward the inside wall

(**fig. b**). Attach it to the inside of the rim, stapling through all of the layers every 4 inches.

5. Finish filling the barrel until the water is just below the staples.

6. Let the water warm up before including plants. Add water conditioner if you have treated water to remove the chlorine, or just wait a few days for it to evaporate naturally.

7. Carefully place your plants in the pond. Position plants at the proper levels with a few cinder blocks, bricks or plastic pots (**fig. c**).

a
b

c

Monarch Caterpillar on Milkweed
Mary Rabadan ~ Annandale, VA

Ruby-Throated Hummingbird at Black and Blue Salvia
Bud Hensley ~ Middleton, OH

Tree Swallow
Michele Thielke ~ Eau Claire, WI

Sulphur Butterfly at Clover
David Sims ~ Versailles, KY

SUMMER *GARDEN* gallery

Take your mind off the sweltering temps
with these cool summertime photos
from fellow outdoor enthusiasts.

Rhododendron
Bernadette Banville ~ Fall River, MA

Bachelor Buttons
Barbara McGiffin ~ Mt. Airy, MD

Ruby-Throated Hummingbird at Butterfly Bush
James Martin ~ Fond du Lac, WI

Blue Butterfly
Jeff Strom ~ Orillia, ON

Swallowtails at Bee Balm
Deanna Mullins ~ Harrison, AR

Eastern Bluebird
Elaine Prince ~ Garrison, TX

show off your work

Shine the spotlight on your photography talents! Join the *birdsandblooms.com* community and upload your digital photos.

in awe of AUTUMN

fall
BACKYARD
checklist

Work your way through this quick list of autumn wildlife garden tasks, and you'll be spotting more birds and butterflies in your yard then ever.

Blazing star is **a whimsical addition** to any garden. The genus *Liatris* offers many choices.

Keep Your Garden Gorgeous

☐ **MAKE** sure you've planted plenty of mums (above), asters and cardinal flowers to tempt fall fliers and brighten your landscape.

☐ **FALL** is a good time to purchase and plant small trees and shrubs, such as conifers, flowering dogwood and redbud. These attract insects for birds in spring, serve as host plants for some butterflies and provide shade and shelter year-round.

☐ **MANY** backyard shrubs and trees, including mountain ash, viburnum and cotoneaster, are laden with birds' favorite berries. Don't have them? Plant one or two for a bumper crop next year.

☐ **DURING** late-autumn garden cleanup, let healthy, pest-free perennials stand. They add beauty to the winter landscape, provide food for birds and are winter homes for desirable insects.

As summer's heat subsides and the days get shorter, it's time to start seasonal chores in the backyard. Stay on track this fall with an easy checklist. Although autumn arrives at different times depending on where you live, nearly everything on the list applies to most regions. Let's roll up our sleeves and get to work!

Amp up Feeder Traffic

☐ **YOU** *can* still get hummingbirds in fall, so don't store your sugar-water feeder until late in the season. Feeding won't interfere with migration, and you just might host a few stragglers.

☐ **SWITCH** to hopper-style feeders, which are more practical than tray feeders at times when the moisture from rain and snow can ruin food. Tube feeders work well in inclement weather, as well.

☐ **DOUBLE** the number of seed and suet feeders around your yard, since there are more mouths to feed in fall.

☐ **CHECK** the condition of your feeders and squirrel baffles to ensure they'll make it through winter. Replace those you can't repair.

DOGWOOD DELIGHTS. If you want a year-round wildlife magnet, look to flowering dogwood. At this time of year, many bird species, including house finches, feast on its shiny red berries.

Notice the Changes

☐ **OBSERVE** your backyard goldfinches. Even though they lose their traditional bright-yellow coloring in fall and winter, they're still out hunting for seed.

☐ **BEFORE** the ground freezes, watch for flickers eating ants and towhees searching for decaying matter.

☐ **EACH** fall, the arrival of juncos is much anticipated and marks the transition from warm to cool weather.

Dark-eyed juncos have white bellies, which you rarely see because they feed on the ground. If you watch closely, you may glimpse a flash of pure white as they fly away.

☐ **KEEP** track of your backyard visitors in a journal. Birds are creatures of habit, so take notes on their behavior patterns: Next fall, you'll have a better idea of what species you'll see and when to look for them.

Welcome Fall Butterflies

☐ **WATCH** for the fall migration of monarchs across the U.S. They will travel in a southerly or southwestern direction, riding the air currents.

☐ **LEAVE** fermenting fall fruit on the ground to attract common buckeyes, California sisters, viceroys and white admirals well into October.

☐ **PREPARE** your butterfly hibernation box for winter. Get rid of any debris and insects inside, wash it and hang it in a safe spot. Set out rotting fruit to entice visitors.

CONNIE ETTER

food for FLIGHT

Give migratory birds the fuel they need by making your backyard a stopover habitat.

BY DAVID MIZEJEWSKI

ON THE MOVE. Many bird species travel in flocks, like the snow buntings pictured here. Snow buntings spend their summers in the northernmost parts of North America and move south for winter.

In fall, birds like this American robin can get **both food and shelter** from dogwoods.

a s cold weather approaches, animals begin to change their behavior in anticipation of the oncoming lean and often harsh winter months. Backyard wildlife like frogs and bats start fattening up for their long winter sleep, while animals that don't hibernate start growing thick coats for protection.

Many other species of backyard wildlife, especially birds, simply avoid winter altogether and head south for much warmer habitats. With a little planning, your garden can serve as a special stopover habitat for these migratory species.

Give 'em Some Energy

Migratory birds fly many thousands of miles to their winter homes, with some going as far as Central or South America. The journey requires an enormous amount of energy, so one of the best ways to attract migrants is to make sure your garden is fully stocked with native plants that provide food.

Fruit-bearing native trees and shrubs produce their berries at the same time birds are migrating through and need them most. The birds benefit from the energy-rich berries and the plants benefit by getting the seeds in the berries distributed by the birds. Similarly, migratory hummingbirds rely on late-blooming native vines, shrubs and perennials for the nectar they provide.

Including a diversity of native plants is also the best way to ensure that your garden is filled with plenty of protein-rich insects for the birds. It's a fact

TRICKS OF THE TRADE. A small pond is like a giant welcome sign to birds flying by your area. If you don't have room for something this big, try a birdbath instead. Keep your sugar-water feeders out as long as possible to attract migrants.

that native plants support many more insects than the exotic ones do.

Check with your local native plant society for a list of fall-producing plants in your region. Another great resource is the Lady Bird Johnson Wildflower Center's website, *wildflower.org*. And don't hesitate to supplement the food provided by these native plants by putting out feeders for seedeaters.

Migratory hummingbirds will also take a much-needed break from their travels to feed at nectar feeder. And don't worry, research shows this doesn't interfere with migration.

The Big Picture

After food, migratory birds need two more things: water and cover. A backyard pond or water garden is a great enticement, especially if you include a shallow area that's only an inch or two deep where the birds can land to take a drink and to bathe. A birdbath will do the job nicely, too.

Finally, migratory species need safe places to take a break and regain their strength. Patches of dense vegetation, especially evergreens, will provide this.

Keep in mind that some of the most common backyard birds, including chickadees, cardinals and sometimes bluebirds, don't migrate and will stick out the winter in your yard. Other species, like dark-eyed juncos and snow buntings, breed in the far north and migrate down to the lower 48 for the winter. So the things you're doing to support migratory species will benefit year-round residents, as well.

don't forget butterflies & dragonflies!

Help these beautiful migratory insects on their seasonal journeys.

Monarch butterflies rely on late-season nectar plants to fuel their migration to Mexico or Central California. See page 112 for our favorite fall garden plans. Dragonflies, on the other hand, need plenty of insect prey.

the magic of
MAPLES
These ornamental trees offer more than just shade.

BY KRIS WETHERBEE

Maples are one of the most beautiful and versatile trees you can grow. Embracing more than 130 species, they range from lofty trees to broad, low shrubs. With an abundance of leaf shapes and colors that transform the autumn scene, there is a maple to fit any landscape need.

One element shared by all maples is wildlife appeal. Maples welcome birds and butterflies with a complete package of food, shelter and nesting sites.

All maples produce wing-shaped fruit known as samaras, whose seeds are eaten by grosbeaks (such as the evening grosbeak at far right), finches and others. The bark and leaves host insects that birds including warblers, bluebirds and nuthatches like to snack on.

Flowers provide nectar for butterflies and hummingbirds as new buds break open in spring.

Some butterflies, such as commas, seek out the sugary sap. Maples also function as caterpillar host plants for giant silk moths, as well as for swallowtail and mourning cloak butterflies.

These well-canopied trees with their masses of leaves make ideal sites for summer shelter. For nesting orioles, robins and warblers, maples are places to put down roots and raise their young.

Maples tolerate a wide range of growing conditions. Though some do need dappled shade around noon to prevent summer's heat from scorching their delicate foliage, most will thrive no matter what the weather brings.

In general, maples grow best in fertile, moist and well-drained soil. The key to a healthy maple is to provide a steady, consistent supply of water throughout the root zone. A 3- to 4-inch layer of organic mulch applied in late spring will help maintain soil moisture while insulating the roots.

our readers share
What is your favorite type of maple tree?

"I like Japanese maples. Too bad they don't fare well here in Wyoming. My daughter has a beautiful one in Seattle."
—CATHY M., *Casper, WY*

"I love the vine maple. It is so lacy looking, and you can use wood chunks for smoking meats, fish and cheeses."
—TERRI S., *via Facebook*

"Red maples are beautiful. I have a huge one in my front yard that shades the house. The birds seem to love it, too. And the leaves are small and easy to mulch after they fall."
—JENNIFER T., *Saint David, IL*

"My all-around favorite is the trident maple (*Acer buergerianum*). It is beautiful in every season!"
—SHEILA ANN G., *Milford, DE*

"Sugar maple is my favorite, not only for its beautiful green foliage, but also the fabulous fall colors and the wonderful maple syrup."
—PAMELA P., *Syracuse, NY*

"The striped maple (*A. pensylvanicum*) is a personal favorite because it's less common than other varieties in my zone."
—ELIZABETH F., *via Facebook*

"Silver maples: When the leaves flip over in the breeze, you know rain is coming."
—MARLA L., *Saint Francis, ME*

"I live in Northern Alberta, and the Amur maple is the only variety with red fall leaves that can survive in our climate."
—TRICIA R., *via Facebook*

American Lady on Dahlia

ATTRACT
MORE *birds &*
butterflies
These plants are irresistible *this fall*
to autumn wildlife.

BUTTERFLY: KALGER; ASTER, CHRYSANTHEMUM, CONEFLOWER: PERENNIALRESOURCE.COM; BLACK-EYED SUSAN: RENEE JORDAN; CELOSIA W. VOLFF BURPEE & CO.; DAHLIA: PROVEN WINNERS, PROVENWINNERS.COM

With the seasonal migration in full swing and local birds and butterflies preparing for winter, now's your chance to host more fliers than ever. Put out the welcome mat with 29 of our favorite autumn all-stars.

annuals, biennials & perennials

Aster
Aster spp. • Zones 3 to 8
A popular cut flower, the aster incites an explosion of color to the end of the growing season. From miniature alpine plants to giants that tower up to 6 feet, asters will brighten fall, especially when the late-season butterflies come to visit. Hundreds of varieties give gardeners plenty of options.

Black-Eyed Susan
Rudbeckia spp. • Zones 3 to 9
Lovely as a background planting or in a wildflower garden, black-eyed Susan also shines when grouped with other daisy-shaped flowers. Plants range from 1 to 6 feet in height, offering a big visual impact in any size yard. Birds love the late-fall seed heads.

Celosia
Celosia argentea • grown as an annual
This velvety favorite doesn't mind heat, so get it going in summer and it will last well into autumn. Available in shades of red, purple, orange and yellow, celosia plants have two different types of flower heads: feathered and spiky, or wavy and flat. The latter resembles a rooster's comb, hence this long-lasting flower's other name, cockscomb. Celosia can thrive in a wide range of soils, including heavy clay.

Chrysanthemum
Chrysanthemum and *Dendranthema*
Zones 4 to 8
Mum's the word for many gardeners in autumn, and with good reason. The chrysanthemum is prized for painting landscapes with dense, vivid color, and its excellent frost tolerance ensures a long and lovely show. When planted in spring or summer, this shrubby tender perennial is often called a hardy mum, because it has time to become established. Planted in fall, mums are grown as annuals.

Coneflower
Echinacea spp. • Zones 3 to 9
Birds, bees and butterflies, such as fritillaries, truly love this perennial! You'll see songbirds pause to nibble the seeds, and butterflies and hummers stopping for its nectar into fall. In winter, the remaining seed heads leave an interesting garden focal point.

Dahlia
Dahlia spp. • Zones 8 to 11
It's no wonder the dahlia is the darling of many gardeners. With thousands of cultivars out there, there are colors, shapes and sizes for everyone. Some varieties easily surpass 5 feet, and the flowers grow as big as dinner plates. Gardeners in cooler climates should dig up the tubers once the plants have died back after frost arrives.

Aster

Chrysanthemum

Black-Eyed Susan

Coneflower

Celosia

Dahlia

False Aster

Japanese Anemone

Fountain Grass

Joe Pye Weed

Goldenrod

Mexican Bush Sage

False Aster 🦋

Boltonia asteroides • Zones 4 to 9
Add a natural look to your yard with false aster, a North American native often seen growing in sunny wetlands and along riverbanks. An eye-catching border backdrop, this perennial's flowers have spindly purple, white or pink petals. The gracefully arching plants grow 2 to 6 feet high. You may want to give false aster a haircut each spring to help keep it in shape.

Fountain Grass 🦋

Pennisetum alopecuroides
Zones 5 to 9
With full tufts of fuzzy, drooping flower spikes that turn into natural birdseed, this ethereal grass seems to be heaven-sent. One or more of its many varieties will add charm to your backyard wildlife habitat. Fountain grass reaches 2 to 5 feet.

Goldenrod 🦋

Solidago spp. • Zones 3 to 9
Light up your autumn garden with goldenrod's wispy yellow blooms, which also make long-lasting cut flowers. Choose a type that's not an aggressive self-seeder, such as Fireworks. That way, you won't have to deadhead as often, and the birds will have fortifying seeds to eat when the weather cools.

Mexican Sunflower

Japanese Anemone 🦋🦋

Anemone x *hybrida* • Zones 4 to 8
Well suited to sun or partial shade, the Japanese anemone produces saucer-shaped white or pink flowers throughout the season. Be sure the site you choose to plant it has moist, humus-rich soil and gets some sun. A fine choice for autumn, it thrives in cool, damp conditions.

Joe Pye Weed 🦋

Eupatorium spp. • Zones 3 to 11
A sun-loving sky-high perennial that needs no staking, this native wildflower is a showstopper when its giant puffs of mauve florets come into bloom. You can find varieties for smaller spaces, too, such as Little Joe and Gateway.

Mexican Bush Sage 🦋

Salvia leucantha • annual to Zone 8
Butterflies and hummingbirds will be clamoring for a space at this plant's late-blooming purplish flowers. In areas where this sage is hardy, it can be established as a shrub. In cooler zones, plant it outdoors as soon as the threat of frost has passed: It needs a long growing season. No matter where you live, grow Mexican bush sage in full sun with moist yet well-draining soil.

Mexican Sunflower 🦋

Tithonia rotundifolia • annual
This fast-growing annual, which blooms in late summer and autumn, reaches 6 feet in height. Its long-lasting orange and red flowers glow in full sun. For smaller spaces, try a compact variety such as Goldfinger or Fiesta Del Sol. Resist the urge to deadhead— songbirds enjoy the seeds.

Despite its classification as an annual, the Mexican sunflower is a prolific seed producer. **Let it self-sow or save the seed heads to plant next year.** You'll keep the butterflies coming with little effort—and no cash!

FALSE ASTER, FOUNTAIN GRASS, SAGE: PROVEN WINNERS - PROVENWINNERS.COM; GOLDENROD, ANEMONE, YEDDAH; PRAGID; MEXICAN SUNFLOWER

Purpletop Vervain 🦋🦋

Verbena bonariensis • annual to Zone 7
Entice fall-flying butterflies with these delicate, long-stemmed purple flowers. People will take notice, too: This plant can grow up to 5 feet tall. Check with your local extension office before planting: It's invasive in some areas.

Sedum 🦋🦋

***Sedum* spp.** • Zones 3 to 10
Many cultivars of this late-season favorite boast bold-hued foliage, ranging from red to purple to gold. Other types of this versatile succulent, including the popular Autumn Joy, have broccoli-shaped light-green flower heads that slowly change to pink and deepen to burgundy; later, the seeds nourish songbirds. Most sedums are hardy in all but the harshest climates.

Sunflower 🦋🦋

Helianthus annuus • annual
There's something about a sunflower's bright face that simply makes you feel good. And when it comes to kids, few plants cause more excitement than these towering blooms, which can soar up to 15 feet! Tiny nectar-producing flower clusters make up the center, attracting butterflies and hummers. It's no secret that the seeds are a favorite among backyard birds.

Turtlehead 🦋🦋

***Chelone* spp.** • Zones 3 to 9
Bring life to partly shady areas with this distinctive fall butterfly magnet. Pink, purple or white flowers bloom on spikes that grow from 16 to 40 inches high. This native plant thrives in moist soil, so it's an ideal addition to a bog garden.

Purpletop Vervain

Sedum

Sunflower

Turtlehead

shrubs&trees

Autumn Sage

Salvia greggii • Zones 6 to 10
Catch migrating hummingbirds with reddish shades of salvia. The annual of this plant (*S. splendens*) has always been a good choice for those flying jewels, so now try adding the perennial version to your garden. Grow this 2- to 3-foot-tall native Texan shrub in a sunny spot in well-drained soil. Want another color? Autumn sage is also available in orange, purple, white and more.

Bigleaf Maple

Acer macrophyllum • Zones 5 to 9
Even if you don't believe bigger is always better, check out this tree, which boasts the largest leaves of any maple—each is up to a foot wide! A year-round winner for wildlife, bigleaf maple attracts bugs that feed migrating and local birds, produces edible seeds and flowers in spring and, at 70 feet tall and wide, offers lots of protection for nesting and roosting. It's a host for the western tiger swallowtail, too.

Black Chokeberry

Aronia melanocarpa • Zones 3 to 9
A lovely and low-maintenance shrub all year, this chokeberry develops bluish-black fruit that songbirds eat in fall and winter. Butterflies like the spring flowers, and some coral hairstreaks use it as a host. Plants grow 3 to 6 feet tall and up to 10 feet wide. They thrive in full sun or part shade and moist, well-draining soil.

Elderberry

Sambucus spp. • Zones 3 to 9
Birds and butterflies alike take shelter among elderberry's branches. The summer flowers entice swallowtails, hairstreaks and hummers, as well as other pollinators, and birds flock to the late-summer and autumn berries. Species range in height from 10 to 20 feet, and cultivars offer colorful foliage, from black to chartreuse.

Hawthorn

Crataegus spp. • Zones 3 to 9
Commonly used as a border tree in backyard landscapes, hawthorn is a wildlife haven that feeds nectar-seeking butterflies in spring and hungry songbirds in fall. Species of this tree thrive in full sun and grow from 20 to 45 feet tall. All hawthorns have appealing burgundy to orange fall color.

Linden

Tilia spp. • Zones 2 to 9
Growing in full sun, some linden types can reach 100 feet tall, offering plenty of shelter for local fliers. In mid-June to early July, the cone-shaped tree produces fragrant white to pale-yellow blooms that invite a host of pollinators, especially bees; later, the flowers yield small nutlike fruit that feeds foraging birds when the weather cools down. Linden's heart-shaped light-green leaves turn a soft butternut-yellow in autumn.

Sumac

Rhus spp. • Zones 2 to 9
Masses of brilliantly hued leaflets and bunches of bristly berries set sumac apart in the fall. Spring flowers beckon to butterflies; later, bluebirds, robins, flickers and others enjoy the fruit. These shrubs (which can range in height from 8 inches to 20 feet tall) are vigorous spreaders, so be sure you pick a site with plenty of room.

Viburnum

Viburnum spp. • Zones 2 to 9
Among the most popular of ornamental shrubs and small trees, members of this genus are sought after for three reasons: They're beautiful, versatile and easy to grow. What's more, the flowers, the foliage and the colorful fruits all contribute to viburnums' year-round beauty. Ample moisture is the only requirement to keep in mind.

Boston Ivy

Clematis

Grape

Virginia Creeper

vines

Boston Ivy
Parthenocissus tricuspidata
Zones 4 to 8
In autumn, this quick-growing vine is bedecked with scarlet, trident-shaped foliage and midnight-blue berries that attract birds. It thrives in sun or shade and looks stunning when covering a wooden fence (it can destroy brickwork). Vines climb to 50 feet.

Clematis
Clematis spp. • Zones 4 to 9
By September, many clematis varieties are petering out, but other species, such as golden (C. tangutica) and sweet autumn clematis (C. terniflora), are at their peak. Either way, clematis is a fall wildlife winner, because once the petals fall, birds seek out the spindly seed clusters.

Grape
Vitis spp. • Zones 2 to 9
This high-sugar fruit provides lots of energy for birds, and a number of sphinx moths use it as a host plant. The woody, deciduous vines grow up to 30 feet long, do best in full sun and produce late-summer and autumn fruit in a variety of sizes and flavors; some are unpalatable to humans.

Virginia Creeper
Parthenocissus quinquefolia
Zones 3 to 9
The deep blue berries on this vigorous grower are an important food source for migrating birds in fall, when Virginia creeper is most gorgeous. The vines grow in sun or shade and can reach 50 feet in length. Keep an eye out for resident Pandora sphinx moths.

seed for free
Early autumn is prime time to mix up a custom seed blend for your feathered friends. The best part? You can honestly say that you grew it yourself!

1. *Observe which blooms the birds frequent in your backyard. Sunflowers, coneflowers and black-eyed Susans are popular candidates.*

2. *Cut the seed heads from the flowers and put them in a paper bag. Tie it shut and hang flower heads upside down (so the dried seeds can fall) for a few weeks. Once they're dry, shake the bag to catch any last seeds.*

3. *Store your mix in a cool, dry place until you're ready to share it.*

FALL *gardens*
FOR BIRDS & BUTTERFLIES

Welcome autumn fliers with these simple planting plans.

Sure, you could plant a few mums or some goldenrod and hope to attract winged friends, but if you transform your yard into a wildlife habitat, your chances of increasing bird and butterfly traffic will soar! Try these three autumnal landscapes.

Brilliant Border

This combo of flowers and foliage expertly ushers in the season, providing both food and shelter for wildlife.

1. **Burning bush** *Euonymus alatus*, Zones 4 to 9
2. **Maiden grass** *Miscanthus sinensis* 'Gracillimus,' Zones 6 to 9
3. **Sneezeweed** *Helenium* spp., Zones 4 to 9
4. **Goldenrod** *Solidago* spp., Zones 2 to 9
5. **Chrysanthemum** *Chrysanthemum* spp. and *Dendranthema* spp., Zones 4 to 8

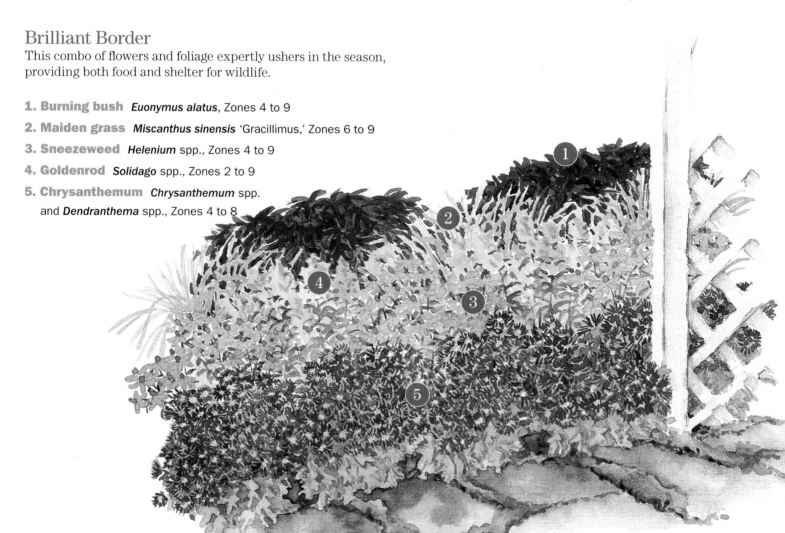

SWAP SHADES.
Want an orange red-hot poker instead of the red one in our plan? Change any element you'd like!

Autumn Splendor

A blend of late-season bird and butterfly favorites is the perfect complement to changing foliage nearby.

1. **Dwarf pampas grass** *Cortaderia selloana*, Zones 7 to 11

2. **Golden clematis** *Clematis tangutica*, Zones 5 to 11

3. **Red-hot poker** *Kniphofia* spp., Zones 4 to 9

4. **Dwarf gloriosa daisy** *Rudbeckia hirta* 'Morena,' Zones 3 to 7

5. **Knotweed** *Persicaria affinis*, Zones 3 to 8

6. **Japanese anemone** *Anemone* x *hybrida*, Zones 4 to 8

Super Shrubbery

These five picks will shine all year, but in autumn they're especially brilliant.

1. **Witch hazel** *Hamamelis* x *intermedia*, Zones 5 to 9

2. **Japanese maple** *Acer palmatum*, Zones 5 to 8

3. **Dwarf heavenly bamboo** *Nandina domestica*, Zones 6 to 11

4. **Oregon grapeholly** *Mahonia aquifolium*, Zones 6 to 9

5. **Flowering quince** *Chaenomeles speciosa*, Zones 5 to 9

PERFECT FALL *planters* FOR WILDLIFE

Sure, summer is over, but gardens are still going strong! Make your autumn landscape extra-alluring with simple yet stellar pots and planters like these.

Belle of the Ball

Count on this buttery-yellow blend to look its best all season—through heat spells and on chilly days.

LIGHT REQUIREMENTS: Sun

POT SIZE: 12 inches

INGREDIENTS:

A. **Butterfly Marguerite daisy**
2 plants

B. **Superbells® Yellow Chiffon calibrachoa** ~ 3 plants

C. **Dolce® Licorice coral bells**
2 plants

D. **Creeping wirevine** ~ 2 plants

Garnet Brocade™ sedum's flowers **make way for seed heads** that remain attractive all winter.

Breezy Meadow

Rich, earthy hues and touchable organic textures make for a quintessentially rustic combination.

LIGHT REQUIREMENTS: Sun

POT SIZE: 12 inches

INGREDIENTS:

A. Ogon golden variegated sweet flag ~ 2 plants

B. 'Black Scallop' bugleweed ~ 1 plant

C. Garnet Brocade™ sedum ~ 1 plant

D. Soprano® White osteospermum ~ 1 plant

Timeless Beauty

Though it's packed into a small container, this arrangement's contrasting colors and textures give it lots of impact.

LIGHT REQUIREMENTS: Sun

POT SIZE: 12 inches

INGREDIENTS:

A. Ogon golden variegated sweet flag ~ 2 plants

B. Superbells® Apricot Punch calibrachoa
2 plants

C. Angelina sedum ~ 2 plants

D. Garnet Brocade™ sedum ~ 2 plants

Jubilee

Plant this vibrant mix in summer to get a head start on the migrators that will flock your yard come fall.

LIGHT REQUIREMENTS: Sun

POT SIZE: 24 inches

INGREDIENTS:

A. Supertunia® Royal Velvet petunia ~ 4 plants

B. Tricolor sage ~ 4 plants

C. Superbena® Coral Red verbena ~ 3 plants

Daydreamer

True-blue flowers and silvery foliage combine to create a wave of color that's enticing to butterflies.

LIGHT REQUIREMENTS: Sun

POT SIZE: 16 inches

INGREDIENTS:

A. Leadwort ~ 3 plants

B. Icicles licorice plant ~ 2 plants

C. Angelina sedum ~ 2 plants

Ornamental Elegance

A pot of easy-to-grow plants like these is sure to please both the gardener and any hungry fliers.

LIGHT REQUIREMENTS: Sun

POT SIZE: 30 inches

INGREDIENTS:

A. Cape Town Blue felicia daisy ~ 2 plants

B. Ritterkreuz ivy ~ 2 plants

C. Pony Tails Mexican feather grass ~ 3 plants

D. Tukana® Scarlet verbena ~ 4 plants

Bright Idea

Pair up these two bold-hued bloomers, and they'll offer nectar in early fall and seeds later on.

LIGHT REQUIREMENTS: Sun

POT SIZE: 14 inches

INGREDIENTS:

A. Zahara Fire zinnia ~ 2 plants

B. Zahara Scarlet zinnia ~ 2 plants

fall BIRDING *basics*

WHO'S THERE?
Birds to look for now.

THE VISITORS: For many species of birds, it's migration time. Look for insect-, nectar- and fruit-eaters such as buntings, tanagers, wrens, orioles and warblers. They'll be flying south to spend winter where it's warm enough to find their favorite foods. Meanwhile, wait to do your fall garden cleanup so passing birds have plenty of natural foods to choose from.

HUMMINGBIRD EXPLOSION: Many of you will see more hummingbirds in early fall than at any other time of year. You might think that you're seeing the same birds every day, but you are likely seeing wave after wave of look-alike migrants as they slowly move on their way south to Latin America. Those who live east of the Mississippi will see mostly migrating ruby-throated hummingbirds. In the West, broad-tailed, black-chinned, rufous and other hummers will stop by, so keep those sugar-water feeders filled!

THE FREQUENT FLIERS: Bluebirds and robins head south in winter, right? Not always. These fliers seem to frequent both the North and the South, thoroughly confusing those of us who think of them solely as spring and summer birds. While their habits may change—they often travel in flocks at this time of year, for instance—many of these birds will stick around in the cold and snow.

HIDDEN SONGBIRDS: As migrants such as warblers and sparrow species begin to fly through your yard in September, thick vegetation can make them difficult to see. Listen closely for unfamiliar birdsongs, and move your birdbath and at least one ground feeder to an open area of your yard to lure these feathered friends into view.

WHAT'S ON THE MENU?
Feeding tips for autumn fliers.

SEEDEATER FAVORITES: You can never go wrong with black-oil sunflower seeds. In fact, most seedeaters, such as cardinals, house finches and black-capped

While all other birds climb upward **in search of food**, the nuthatch does the exact opposite.

Attract the most birds to your backyard this autumn. BY ANNE SCHMAUSS

chickadees, prefer it. If you do want to add some white millet to your mix, make sure that it makes up no more than 10 to 15 percent. It will get kicked to the ground by messy birds, but that's just fine for juncos and native sparrows, because they prefer to eat their meals on the ground, anyway.

SUET SEASON: High-fat, high-calorie suet is the perfect food to help birds get through longer nights and colder temperatures. Hang your suet feeder in a tree near a window so you can watch nuthatches, woodpeckers, chickadees and others enjoy this high-energy treat.

NYJER FANATICS: Don't forget the goldfinches. Even though they lose their traditional gold coloring in fall and winter, they are still out there and looking for food. Keep your nyjer (thistle) feeders full, and you just might see a burst of fall activity. The black, rice-shaped seed is grown in Africa and South Asia and has a thin shell that finches quickly and expertly remove. Store it in a cool, dry place.

IN A NUTSHELL
Pressed for time? Follow the basics.

SEED: Keep a healthy supply of sunflower seeds—with and without the shell—on hand at all times, and add suet to your menu to help birds prepare for winter. Don't cut down your nectar-producing flowers just yet—hummers will likely stop by.

WATER: Birds need water every day, even when it's cold outside. Add an electric deicer to your birdbath, or buy one with a built-in heater.

FOOD AND SHELTER: An overgrown yard is bird-friendly. Don't cut back flowers with seed heads or shrubs with berries—they offer great shelter and food! This is also a time to plant trees and shrubs, which will add shelter later.

FLYING SOUTH: Birds that migrate are hardwired to move when the time is right; feeding them does not keep them from going south. So keep your feeders out as long as you want.

GETTING PREPARED. In fall, birds are busily getting ready for winter, whether they're heading south, like yellow-rumped warblers (left) and orchard (far left) and Baltimore (above) orioles; staying put, such as white-breasted nuthatches (top); or still deciding, like eastern bluebirds (center).

Monarch

YEAR-ROUND
butterflies:
AUTUMN

Learn how butterflies prepare for the cooler days ahead. BY KENN KAUFMAN

For most North American butterflies, autumn is less a distinct season than a long goodbye to summer, with its bountiful fields and gardens, before the onset of winter.

Promising a Future

Most adult butterflies will perish before winter arrives. Long before the intense cold weather sets in, the females will have laid eggs, ensuring a new generation for the following year.

With that taken care of, the adults may spend the rest of their short lives wandering in a seemingly aimless way. But some types of adult butterflies do live through the winter, hibernating in sheltered sites, and they may be seeking out such roosting spots as fall advances. Mourning cloaks, question marks, commas and tortoiseshells are among these hibernators, so if you see them flitting about woodpiles or tree cavities in fall, they are likely looking for winter shelter.

Taking Flight

A few varieties fly only in late summer and fall. The red-bordered satyr, which flies floppily through Southwestern canyons in September, is one; another is Leonard's skipper, a denizen of Northeastern meadows. Few of these show up in gardens, so most of the fall activity we see is a continuation of summer behavior, including the northward push of southern species. Subtropical creatures like large pale cloudless sulphurs and tiny orange fiery skippers may still be flying north in early October, even filtering into southern Canada.

But the most distinctive fall movement of butterflies is the southward flight of the monarchs. In spring and summer, generations of monarchs fly north, away from their wintering grounds. The early-fall generation of adults will have a different instinct: to fly south. Through a kind of inherited memory that is as mysterious as it is remarkable, they will return to the same wintering sites that their great-great-grandparents left a few months earlier. We may not understand how they do it, but we can enjoy the spectacle. At some places, such as Point Pelee in southern Ontario, massive numbers of monarchs may gather before continuing their amazing journey.

GLAD YOU ASKED

Find answers to your fall wildlife garden queries here, courtesy of bird, butterfly and plant experts.

MYSTERY HUMMINGBIRD FLOWER

This perennial (left) grows 7 to 8 feet tall and has **numerous scarlet blossoms** on it. It starts blooming in August and continues to flower until the first frost. Can you tell me what it is?

—PATTI J., *Norris, TN*

MELINDA MYERS: Your mystery plant is a Turk's cap (*Malvaviscus arboreus* var. *drummondii*). This Texas and Mexico native is hardy in Zone 7 and warmer. It grows as a small shrub in warmer climates and dies back to the ground, acting similar to a perennial plant.

Grow this heat-tolerant plant in almost any type of soil, in sun or shade. The red flowers attract hummingbirds, butterflies and moths, while the red fruit is relished by a variety of birds.

MULTITASKING TREE

I'd like to plant a deciduous tree near my deck. Can you suggest one that **flowers and produces berries** that birds enjoy?

—LOTTIE E., *Rapid City, SD*

MELINDA: Look for a tree that's suitable to your growing conditions, hardy to your area and doesn't create a mess with its fruit.

Serviceberry (botanically known as *Amelanchier*) is tolerant of partial shade and hardy in Zones 2 to 9. It produces blueberry-like fruit that the birds will pick clean off the tree. The size varies with the cultivar selected.

European mountain ash (*Sorbus aucuparia*) grows 20 to 40 feet tall, prefers cool, moist soils in the summer and is hardy in Zones 3 to 7. Many birds, but especially cedar waxwings, enjoy its fruit.

A close relative that best tolerates hot, dry summers is the Korean mountain ash (*Sorbus alnifolia*). Hardy in Zones 4 to 7, it can reach heights of 40 feet. It has bright, pinkish-red fruit and beautiful fall color.

And don't forget about crabapples (a member of the *Malus* genus). Select cultivars are bred for their disease resistance and persistent fruit. Some, like Birdland, are especially attractive to birds. Visit a reliable nursery to find the cultivar that best suits your needs.

Turn the page for bird and butterfly advice.

FAMILY WANTED

We have several suet feeders in the cherry tree that's in front of our bay window. Our newest visitor is a female downy woodpecker. **We want to attract a mated pair.** Will this be enough to hold their attention as a nesting site?

—JUDY B., *Port Huron, MI*

GEORGE HARRISON: Since you've seen the female downy (like this one), at least you know the suet feeder is enough to attract these woodpeckers. So now it might just be a matter of patience. I would guess that a male will eventually arrive, and then with luck juveniles will be at your suet next.

If you don't have many trees around, it's doubtful that you'll get the family to nest in your yard. But if you keep your feeders out, at least they'll know where they are guaranteed a meal. Some woodpeckers, including downies, will use a nesting box if it has the right dimensions. Search for "birdhouse guidelines" on *birdsandblooms.com* to learn more.

SEALED SHUT

When we saw this hummingbird (right), it **appeared as if its bill was cemented shut.** We carefully ran its bill under warm water and scraped the stickiness off it. Soon, its bill opened, and its tongue started to flicker. We let it go, and it drank from the feeders. What was wrong with it?

—LISA M., *Savanna, IL*

GEORGE: It is common for hummingbirds to eat the sap from evergreen trees. In fact, hummingbirds often tap the holes that sapsucker woodpeckers drill because they find insects that are attracted to the sap.

My guess is that this hummingbird got into too much sap, and had its bill sealed shut. The warm water was a good idea. You likely saved its life!

AUTUMN BLUES

Every fall these **pretty blue beauties** show up in our yard. They flutter away as quickly as they land, but one day I was able to snap this photo (above). Can you tell me what they are?

—TERESA K., *Grandview, WA*

TOM ALLEN: You've discovered the common checkered skipper, a butterfly that has two broods—one in spring and another in late summer and early fall. The butterfly's blue appearance comes from long, bluish hairs on the inner part of the wings. The species prefers fields and pastures with low-growing mallows, where it feeds.

The caterpillars of this butterfly make leaf nests by rolling or attaching a group of leaves together with silk near the top of mallow plants. The nests are fairly easy to find. If you carefully look inside, you will see the greenish caterpillar, with a dark head and covered with short, whitish hairs. The caterpillars will winter fully grown in these leaf shelters.

BIRDS WON'T EAT BERRIES

Several years ago, **we planted two American cranberry bush shrubs** in our yard because we heard that they attract wild birds. The birds won't touch the berries. Why?

—LINDA H., *Redford, MI*

GEORGE: I don't know why your birds avoid the berries of your American cranberry bush. It is one of the best shrubs you can plant for birds. It produces an especially good crop of red berries that cedar waxwings, American robins, gray catbirds and northern cardinals crave.

Perhaps you have a variety of the plant that is different than most. Overall, any native hawthorns, crabapples, dogwoods or ash trees are excellent fruit-producing plants that should attract birds.

Wood is **the best material for birdhouses**. Cover it with whatever you like.

BACKYARD BUILDERS

What's more cozy and rustic than a log cabin in autumn? These woodworkers scaled theirs down with feathered friends in mind.

^ LAKESIDE LEISURE "I enjoy making bluebird houses that resemble log cabins, so I thought I'd try a log feeder," Joe Blackwell of Lake Wylie, South Carolina, tells us. "The most intricate work was the roof—each shingle is hand cut and individually placed."

^ STYLISH SLATE Stone homes can be just as warm and welcoming as log ones. "Since my husband retired, he's been busy building birdhouses. So when a friend brought him some leftover slate tiles, he used them to construct this," explains Joyce Whipple of Garden Grove, California. "Those colorful flat stones make quite a distinctive look."

< PART OF THE NEIGHBORHOOD "My neighbor George Szucs has a lovely, parklike yard," says Lynn Tait of Summerland, British Columbia. "This is one of his birdhouses. It's very unique and comes equipped with hinges and a doorknob!"

< CABIN CAFE Rhoda Hreha of Alexandria, Ohio, shared this sturdy bird feeder made by her brother, Francis Wallace. "The end of the seed tray unhooks, so it's easy to clean out the leftover shells from the bottom," she says. "Best of all, the birds love the protection the roof gives them."

< PERFECT FOR A PIT STOP This feeder boasts bells and whistles in form and function. "My husband, Charlie, built it for our friends who live in Canada," says Karen Chatman, who's from Canadian Lakes, Michigan. "The roof is hinged, so it's easy to refill the seed."

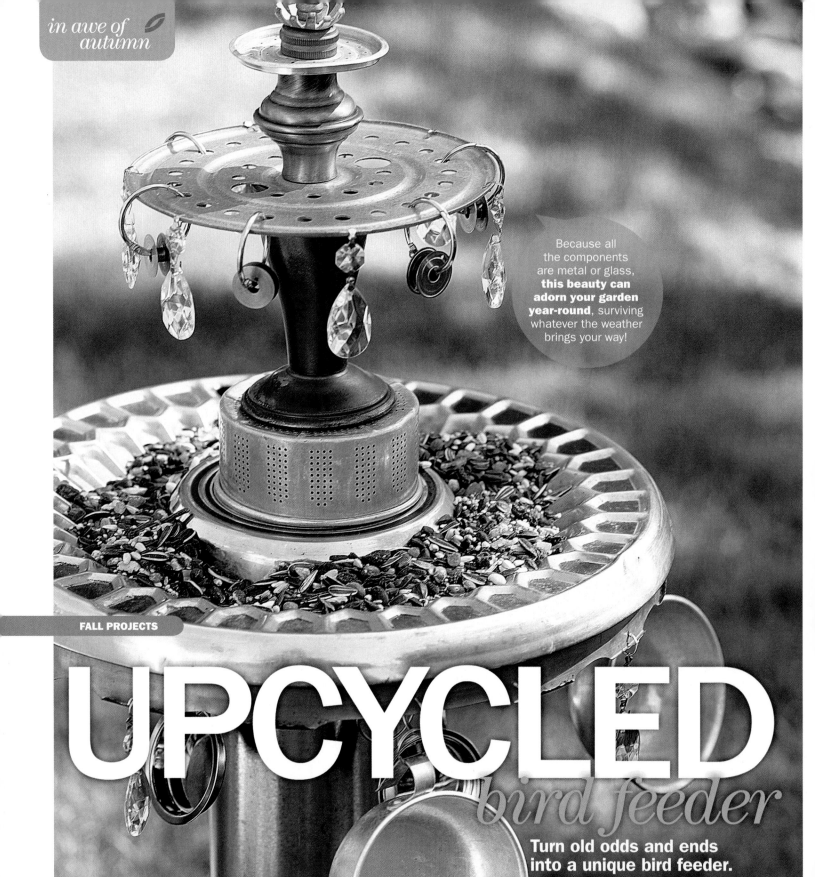

Because all
the components
are metal or glass,
**this beauty can
adorn your garden
year-round**, surviving
whatever the weather
brings your way!

FALL PROJECTS

UPCYCLED
bird feeder

**Turn old odds and ends
into a unique bird feeder.**

BY BETH EVANS-RAMOS

This fancy feeder will give birds something to tweet about.

YOU DON'T HAVE TO SPEND A LOT OF MONEY to have an interesting bird feeder. Just look around your house for a few items that are begging to be repurposed; then put them together for a whimsical piece of functional garden art.

Here, crystal chandelier drops add elegance, plumbing parts lend an industrial touch and the old hubcap that holds the seed is pure recycled genius!

While a feeder built using this concept can take many different shapes, here are some basic steps to help you fashion one of your own. It will be 100-percent unique.

1. To begin, look for items to stack that may already have holes or openings in the center.

2. You will likely need to punch or drill a hole in the center of your hubcap, just big enough for your threaded rod to slip through. Also make a hole in any other piece that needs a center opening.

3. Experiment with stacking your metal pieces. Just start on a flat surface and layer away. It's fun to have a piece to hang things from underneath your hubcap; try an upside-down vegetable steamer for a playful look.

4. Once you create a combination you like, take one of the metal nuts and thread it onto the rod about one foot below the top. Slide on your bottom piece and add another nut for a secure base.

5. Next, add the hubcap and the other pieces. The best part of this project is that you can change your mind as often as you want!

6. To finish your stack, slip on the third metal nut and tighten it until your pieces stay securely side by side. You might have to adjust the bottom nuts either higher or lower along the rod.

7. If you don't want the top nut to show, glue on a finial, such as a hose connector (***fig. a***). Use a sturdy, waterproof glue.

8. It's time to decorate with dangling embellishments! Suspend camping cups, crystal chandelier drops, beads, sewing bobbins, mystery parts or whatever you fancy from the built-in openings or through holes punched around the edges (***fig. b***).

Easy connectors are large paper clips, split rings or binder rings. At first, your feathered friends might be nervous around the accessories, but give them some time and they'll get used to the new additions.

9. Your threaded rod will slip inside a section of pipe, which can be placed in a garden pot or a flower bed. If you want a freestanding bird feeder, the rod can slip into the base and pole taken from a socket-free, semi-disassembled floor lamp.

10. The only thing left to do is add the bird treats!

WHAT YOU NEED

Metal punch, drill or hammer and nail

Threaded rod

3 metal nuts that fit the threaded rod

A section of pipe or the bottom portion of a floor lamp (for the base)

Hubcap, the older the better

Kitchen steamer

Lamp parts

Coffee percolator parts

Garden hose connections

Waterproof glue, such as Amazing Goop

Dangling embellishments

Connectors for embellishments

a

b

Be sure to **read the paint can instructions before you start** so you can allow adequate time for drying.

WHAT YOU NEED

Vent (shanty) cap

Drill

Aluminum pie plate

Exterior primer and paint (optional)

1/4-inch eyebolt

1/4-inch hex head cap screw

1/4-inch coupling nut

Wrench

Superglue

Twine or wire for hanging

PIE TIN *bird feeder*

You don't need a lot to create this durable feeder.

BY JENNIFER MANCIER

IF YOU'RE LOOKING FOR A BIRD FEEDER that will stand the test of time, this one is for you. A vent (shanty) cap protects the food while a pie plate or a round cake pan presents a picnic for your backyard birds. You can easily obtain all the supplies from a hardware store, but also look for vintage pie or cake pans at yard sales and consignment shops. Then each feeder you make will be one of a kind!

1. Wearing safety glasses, drill a 5/16-inch hole through the center of the vent cap and the pie plate.

2. While you're at it, drill a few small holes through the bottom of the pie plate to allow for water drainage.

3. Leave the vent cap and pie plate bare for an industrial look, or use paint to add a pop of color! I find that a latex-based exterior paint over primer sticks best to galvanized metal.

Paint the vent cap and pie plate separately before assembling your feeder.

4. Choose an eyebolt and cap screw that have a combined height of 1/8 inch to 3/4 inch less than the height of the vent cap. That way, there will be just enough room for the coupling nut to hold the two together tightly.

Place the cap screw through the center hole in the pie plate with the threads facing upward.

5. Thread the coupling nut onto the cap screw, turning the nut 3 to 4 times to hold it in place.

6. Next, center the vent cap over the pie plate while holding the cap screw still.

7. Thread the eyebolt through the center hole of the vent cap and turn the eyebolt into the other end of the coupling nut. Using a wrench, hold the nut steady while hand-tightening the eyebolt. Dab a few drops of superglue onto the coupling nut for extra holding power.

8. To hang, slip twine or wire through the eyehole and tie.

9. Hang the filled feeder from a branch and watch as the birds gather 'round to enjoy your new backyard masterpiece!

hummingbird FEEDER *for pennies*

Give yourself the best view in the house, especially during migration seasons. BY LISA SZCZYGIEL-DURANTE

WHAT YOU NEED

12 inches of 18-gauge copper wire

1/2-inch suction cup with a hole in the base

Plastic test tube with cap

Decorative beads (optional)

Artificial flower, with stem removed

Small wire cutters

Pliers (for twisting and spiraling wire)

I LOVE SEEING HUMMINGBIRDS UP CLOSE, so I designed a feeder just for that purpose. This window feeder is simple, but it certainly does the job. Best of all, once hummingbirds are used to feeding from it, you can remove it from the base and feed them by hand!

1. Cut an 8-inch piece from the copper wire. Let the wire naturally take a half-moon shape.

2. Lace 2 inches of the wire through the hole in the suction cup and then fold and twist the wire until it's secure.

3. Gently bend the longer end of the wire into an arc, leaving 3/4 inch at the very end for the hook that will attach to the feeder.

Visit Lisa's site, *hum-fi.com*, to **learn tricks for hand-feeding hummingbirds** with your mini feeder.

4. With pliers, make a large loop at the end of the arc, forming a hook, with the open end on the top or facing up. This will make it easier to attach the feeding tube quickly and will prevent the feeder from falling off.

5. Take the remaining 4 inches of copper wire and wrap it around the test tube, leaving one end much longer than the other. Use pliers to twist and secure the wire to the test tube. This should leave a 3/4-inch tail remaining to attach a decorative glass bead.

6. Slide the ring more than halfway up the tube, so that when full, the feeder will stay upright.

7. Slide another bead onto the open end of the wire wrapped around the tube and use the pliers to spiral the wire and close it up completely. Now the copper wire should be wrapped firmly around the feeding tube and you have

a loop to attach to your hook with the suction cup.

8. Make a small hole in the tube's cap, secure it on the tube and poke the end of the artificial flower through the hole so that the hummingbirds can reach the nectar as naturally as possible. Poke a hole in the flower's center if necessary.

9. Attach the closed loop on the tube to the upward-facing shepherd's hook with the suction cup. Make sure your window is clean so the suction cup will be secure.

10. Ta-da! A nifty little hummingbird feeder. Place it in a window where you can easily view it.

Japanese Maple Leaves
Helen Bitaxis ~ Sewickley, PA

Anna's Hummingbird
Sam Wilson ~ Scottsdale, AZ

Dark-Eyed Junco
Michael Sargent ~ Middleport, NY

Acorns
Tami Kelso ~ Conway, AR

AUTUMN GARDEN
gallery

Mother Nature's finest fall offerings
are featured in these shots shared
by *Birds & Blooms* readers.

Bohemian Waxwings
Robert Morin ~ Quebec, QC

Eastern Bluebird
George Slattery ~ Williamsport, PA

Comma Butterfly
Alice Behn ~ Preston, IA

Persimmons
Kathy Rowland ~ Mattoon, IL

Chestnut-Backed Chickadee
Dan Garber ~ Troy, MT

Squirrel
Linda Hoopes ~ Indianapolis, IN

come join us

Get in on the photo fun! As a member of *birdsandblooms.com*, you can submit your own original images.

wonders of WINTER

winter BACKYARD *checklist*

Keep the wildlife coming in rain, snow, sleet or hail with our cold-weather checklist.

Collect photos of plants you love. When you can, **label the images** so you know what to look for at the nursery.

Plan Your Best Garden Yet

☐ **RING** in the New Year by starting a garden journal that chronicles Mother Nature's doings in your yard, from what's growing to who's visiting to what the weather's like.

☐ **PERUSE** seed catalogs, garden magazines (such as *Birds & Blooms*), the Web and other resources to decide what leafy wildlife magnets you would like to purchase and plant for the next growing season.

☐ **DESIGN** a new garden with an eye to attracting birds and butterflies. Be sure to plant varieties that are useful year-round, whether for food or even shelter.

Although winter's arrival offers a chance to give your rake a rest, there's still plenty to do and see. Take this time to feed birds, study up on local butterflies and plan for next year's garden. Whether you live in sunny Florida or snowy Alberta, you're sure to find these helpful tips worth tackling.

Focus on the Food

☐ **TITMICE** (right), brown creepers, chickadees, jays and woodpeckers all love peanut pieces. Add some to your seed mix, or hang a special peanut feeder to attract extra attention.

☐ **ENERGY-BOOSTING** suet is the ideal food to help birds survive winter's longer nights and colder temps. Place a suet feeder right outside your window for prime in-home viewing.

☐ **AFTER** the holidays, place your Christmas tree in the backyard to give birds a convenient cover. Continue the festivities by hanging up seed ornaments and other treats.

☐ **PUT** out a seed block or cake, making sure it's loaded with high-fat foods like sunflower seeds and nuts (but skip the less-popular fillers such as millet and milo).

☐ **KEEP** berry- and seed-bearing plants snow- and ice-free.

Brush up on Butterflies

☐ **LOCATE** a regional butterfly field guide and read all about the species that live in or pass through your region. In the coming months, you'll be able to identify and attract these flying flowers.

☐ **ORDER** butterfly- and bird-attracting plants now to avoid the spring rush. Companies will generally wait to deliver them until the time is right to plant in your region.

☐ **EVEN** if there's still patchy snow, be ready to spot mourning cloaks in late winter.

WORRY-FREE BATHS. There's no need to be concerned about birds (such as these mourning doves) freezing in icy water. Our expert, George Harrison, says they'll drink from a heated birdbath, but if it's too cold, birds won't bathe or even get their feathers wet.

Care for Backyard Birds

☐ **ROBINS** and bluebirds don't always head south in winter. While their habits may change—they often travel in flocks this time of year—many of the birds stick around in cold and snow.

☐ **SNOW** and ice storms greatly increase birds' vulnerability. Keep your feeders clear, and dedicate a spot for ground feeding.

☐ **LOOK** for winter irrupters such as evening grosbeaks, crossbills, redpolls and pine siskins—birds known to flock outside their usual habitats.

☐ **BIRDS** need water every day, even when it's cold out. Buy a heated birdbath or add an electric de-icer to one you already own.

JOURNAL: RDA-GID; GARDEN PLAN: SCOTT E. FEUER / SHUTTERSTOCK.COM; TITMOUSE: SCHAYDEN; BATH: BOB O'DEAN

CARDINALS: MASLOWSKI WILDLIFE; GOLDFINCH: JUDY CREPEAU

CHILLING OUT. When the weather cools, northern cardinals flock, abandoning their territorial instincts. Goldfinches molt into an understated set of feathers.

WINTER
wonderland

Provide a warm welcome to your feathered friends this winter in only three easy steps. BY DAVID SHAW

i spend a lot of time thinking about winter birds. In Fairbanks, Alaska, where I live, the handful of species that survive the dark winters are forced to deal with extreme cold and little daylight. They are remarkable creatures and are beautifully adapted to their environment. They remind me that there is life in the woods.

Birds, like humans, need only a few things to survive the winter—food, water and shelter—all of which are readily available in the wild. The trick to drawing birds into your yard, though, is to make offerings superior to what they can find elsewhere.

No matter how cold the winters are where you live, see the following pages for tricks to get the most visitors to your yard.

KEYS TO SURVIVAL. A blue jay (below) visits a heated birdbath. Peanut butter is a favorite food for many birds, including black-capped chickadees (right). Festive and functional bird houses like these (far right) offer safe roosting spots.

1. Food

As at all times of year, quality food is the most important aspect of any bird-friendly backyard. But good bird feeding is, unfortunately, not as straightforward as hanging a feeder in a nearby tree. Here are some things to think about:

FOOD DIVERSITY: Different bird species prefer different types of food. Here in Alaska, black-oil sunflower seeds and peanut butter are sure favorites, while millet will remain uneaten in the feeder. In other parts of the country, the opposite could be true.

Start out by providing a variety of foods to see what your local species prefer. Suet, sunflower seeds, dried and fresh fruit, and even mealworms can make excellent bird food.

FEEDER VARIETY: Birds vary their foraging locations. Some fliers, like woodpeckers, prefer to forage while gripping vertically to the side of the tree or feeder. Others, such as chickadees and finches, favor horizontal perches. Juncos and other sparrows often will choose the ground, or flat, platform-style feeders.

CONSISTENCY: If you are new to feeding, it may take a few days for birds to find your feeding station, but once they do, they will return again and again. Keeping your feeders full is important. A few days of empty feeders and the birds will quickly disappear for better foraging areas.

2. Water

Water can be a great way to make your yard stand out. Consider these ideas:

PONDS: Birds are accustomed to getting their water from ground-level ponds, puddles and creeks. A small backyard pond with recirculating water is easy to build and is preferred by many birds. If you live in the North, your pond will likely freeze over for winter. But if your area stays above freezing most of the time, a pond would be a welcoming addition to your backyard.

BIRDBATHS: These are usually elevated and can seem unnatural for some cautious species. However, baths have two notable advantages: ease and the ability to have heated water in winter. Some water is better than none, and heated birdbaths will keep the water unfrozen if your winter temperatures slip below freezing.

3. Shelter

Shelter is important to birds throughout the year. If you provide protection from weather, cold and predators, your yard will quickly become an especially appealing place.

DEFENSE: Small birds are hesitant to cross large open areas. This exposes them to predators that may be lurking in the sky above or on the ground below. Avoid this hesitancy by placing your feeders close to trees and shrubs. (Species native to your

area will be more appealing than ornamentals.)

COVER: Dense shrubs and trees also provide space for birds to protect themselves from the wind and weather. Evergreens that retain their foliage through the winter are perfect choices. Pines, spruces, junipers or rhododendrons are excellent choices depending on where you live.

WARMTH: Where I live in Alaska, one of the biggest challenges facing winter birds is keeping warm. Some species, like the black-capped chickadee, use tree cavities to get out of the cold during the long nights. If you have dead trees where woodpeckers have hollowed out holes, leave them in place. Additionally, chickadees will use old birdhouses or even specially made "roosting boxes." If you live in an extreme environment, consider this addition to your backyard bird habitat.

Sometimes I fool myself into believing that without the food and shelter I provide, "my birds" wouldn't survive the winter. But really, as a scientist and naturalist, I know differently.

If I put my feeders away, the birds would just head back to the forest as they have for millennia. Instead, I do it for me. I feed them because their antics and energy make me smile on brutal winter days. I provide for them because I love their presence in my own backyard.

Many people wonder when they should **clean winter birdhouses and nest boxes**. Expert George Harrison suggests waiting till spring—the old nesting materials inside will help insulate against chilly temps.

the best plant picks for
WINTER WILDLIFE

Bohemian Waxwing

Keep birds safe and well fed throughout the coldest months of the year.

In winter, while much of nature has taken time off to re-energize, backyard birds are as active as ever. Give your feathered friends plenty to eat with berry- and seed-bearing plants, plus ample shelter courtesy of evergreens. Here are 25 winter-worthy plants.

perennials

Feather Reed Grass

Calamagrostis x *acutiflora*
Zones 4 to 9
This plant's tall, sweeping, upright habit gives it textural winter eye appeal, while the birds enjoy the seeds. In fact, this drought-tolerant grass is handsome almost year-round: Starting in summer, its green foliage is topped by plush silvery-bronze to purple flowers that persist into snowy weather.

Johnny-Jump-Up

Viola tricolor • Zones 3 to 9
This old-fashioned classic produces a plethora of charming flowers. Plants from seeds sown the previous spring will bloom in fall and often hang on through winter. Johnny-jump-up thrives in pots, so gardeners in cooler climates can help blooms last by bringing the planter inside when temperatures drop. They can enjoy the cheery display even during a blizzard!

Miscanthus

Miscanthus sinensis • Zones 4 to 9
You'll be on cloud nine with the fluffy frosted tops of this ornamental grass. The big, showy flower heads and height of up to 12 feet give it a profile that's both dramatic and graceful. In fall, some plants' silky gray panicles turn maroon or purplish-brown—all last through winter. Plant miscanthus in a sun-drenched area.

Switchgrass

Panicum virgatum • Zones 4 to 9
This fuss-free and versatile ornamental is a smart pick for wet or dry conditions or partial shade, as long as it's planted in well-draining soil. Growing narrow and upright with a pouf of seed heads in fall, switchgrass can reach more than 5 feet tall. Birds take advantage of the thick growing habit and use it for winter cover, and satyrs and skippers use it as a host.

Winter Heath

Erica carnea • Zones 5 to 7
Through most of the winter and into early spring, this reliable, low-growing plant puts on an attractive show of small urn-shaped purple-pink flowers. Songbirds like the cover, and early-arriving butterflies stop by for nectar. Plant it in acidic soil.

Johnny-jump-up is a short-lived perennial, but it's often **planted in fall and treated as a cool-weather annual**. This hardy member of the violet family looks lovely when peeking out from a blanket of fresh snow.

Feather Reed Grass

Switchgrass

Johnny-Jump-Up

Miscanthus

Winter Heath

Barberry · Boxwood · Colorado Blue Spruce · Beautyberry · Camellia · Common Bearberry

shrubs & trees

Barberry
Berberis spp. • Zones 3 to 8
This thorny shrub is grown for its abundant foliage in spring, summer and fall and will provide much-needed shelter for birds in cold weather. For the best color and fruit, grow your barberry in full sun. Try it as a hedge. Barberry will attract bluebirds, gray catbirds, northern mockingbirds, brown thrashers and others.

Beautyberry
Callicarpa spp. • Zones 5 to 8
For a berry bush that's a little unusual, try beautyberry. Its spring or summer flowers are alluring to butterflies, and its fall fruit lasts well into winter in some regions. In others, especially the South, winter songbirds devour the bright-purple berries. This fast-growing shrub will reach about 4 feet tall.

Boxwood
Buxus spp. • Zones 5 to 9
A top choice among landscapers for hedges and topiaries, this evergreen is covered in masses of green or variegated foliage and thrives in sites with partial shade. Because its structure is so dense, it offers ample protection to winter songbirds. Many slow-growing cultivars reach just 5 feet.

Camellia
Camellia spp. • Zones 6 to 11
A popular Southern evergreen, camellia flowers in the fall, winter or early spring, depending on the variety. Camellias are ideal for landscaping and produce beautiful rose-shaped blooms, usually in red, pink or white. Birds will appreciate the shrub for the shelter it provides. Expect camellia to be anywhere from 3 to 20 feet high.

Colorado Blue Spruce
Picea pungens • Zones 3 to 8
Our feathered friends love the thick branches and prickly needles that offer winter shelter, whether it's from stormy weather or nearby predators. Blue spruce cones also produce seed for food. This tree does best in full sun and grows up to 60 feet tall, but dwarf cultivars are readily available, as well.

Common Bearberry
Arctostaphylos uva-ursi • Zones 2 to 6
Rocky and sandy soils are best for this hardy, low-growing evergreen ground cover, making it a good choice for drought-tolerant gardens. Bearberry, also known as kinnikinick, produces tiny white or pink flowers in spring and summer, and long-lasting bright-red berries in fall. It's also a host plant to some elfins and fritillaries.

BARBERRY: SOCK1979; BEAUTYBERRY, COTONEASTER, FIRETHORN: RDA-GID; BOXWOOD, BLUE SPRUCE, BEARBERRY, BARBERRY,

Coralberry

Dogwood

Eastern White Pine

Cotoneaster

Eastern Arborvitae

Firethorn

Coralberry
Symphoricarpos* x *doorenbosii
Zones 2 to 7
With berries in hues of pink and purple, this hybrid is decorative in gardens and delicious for birds. Bushes reach 6 feet tall and thrive in full sun. Prune coralberry in early spring: You'll encourage new growth and see an abundance of berries the following year.

Cotoneaster
***Cotoneaster* spp.** • Zones 3 to 11
Whether they're deciduous, evergreen or semi-evergreen shrubs or trees, cotoneasters sport red and orange berries that songbirds love. They grow in full sun to partial shade in fertile, well-draining soil and range from 1 to 15 feet tall. In summer, you may notice butterflies sampling nectar from the white flowers.

Dogwood
***Cornus* spp.** • Zones 2 to 8
Want a wildlife garden showstopper? Look no further. These berry-rich garden favorites feed robins, bluebirds, cardinals and dozens of other backyard birds during the cold months. Butterflies and other pollinators stop by while the shrubs are flowering, while some species are hosts, as well. Dogwoods do best in full sun to partial shade.

Eastern Arborvitae
Thuja occidentalis • Zones 3 to 7
This tree is dense, with a pyramidal shape and clusters of small seed-bearing cones. It has a classic conifer look (but can be pruned to any shape you want) and provides generous coverage for birds. Plus, nurseries offer plenty of cultivars to choose from. But beware: Deer love it, too.

Eastern White Pine
Pinus strobus • Zones 4 to 9
With long green needles and a quick growing habit, eastern white pine is a good choice for any yard, particularly sunny ones. It reaches 50 to 80 feet tall and 20 to 40 feet wide, so its verdant silhouette is sure to stand out in winter. The deep branches are hospitable to birds during harsh weather, and the cones are a go-to food source for nuthatches and many other seedeaters.

Firethorn
Pyracantha coccinea • Zones 5 to 9
Though it has glossy green foliage for most of the year, it's the compact bunches of pea-size red, orange or yellow berries that get all the attention. The spring or summer flowers are sought after by nectaring butterflies.

Hemlock

Mahonia

Rugosa Rose

Juniper

Mountain Ash

Winterberry

Hemlock

Tsuga spp. • Zones 4 to 8
Hemlock trees are shade-tolerant—especially when they're young—and make good hedges. One variety in particular, Cole's Prostrate Canada hemlock (*T. canadensis*), shown here, has a weeping silhouette with a low, spreading habit and cascading branches. It provides dense shelter for ground-feeding birds such as towhees and juncos.

Juniper

Juniperus spp. • Zones 2 to 9
Also known as redcedars, these trees can grow up to 50 feet tall. A juniper will serve as a secure roosting and nesting site. Some birds, including waxwings, enjoy the berry-like cones, as well. Plant juniper in fall so its roots have time to become established before winter.

Mahonia

Mahonia spp. • Zones 5 to 11
This evergreen shrub has spiny-edged leaves that often resemble those of holly, and bears clusters of blue-black berries. Various species grow from 1 to 12 feet in full sun to light shade. This shrub's yellow flowers emerge early, providing nectar for overwintering hummingbirds and butterflies.

Mountain Ash

Sorbus spp. • Zones 2 to 7
A smart landscaping pick for compact backyards, this medium-size ornamental tree boasts spectacular yellow and red fall foliage. The red or orange berry clusters attract flocks of cedar waxwings, robins, gray catbirds, eastern bluebirds, thrashers and at least a dozen other species. Mountain ash is also a host plant for eastern tiger swallowtails.

Rugosa Rose

Rosa rugosa • Zones 2 to 8
Love roses but hate the hassle? This fast-growing species flourishes virtually anywhere and reaches up to 8 feet tall. Rugosa roses handle poor soil conditions, from sandy to salty, and produce bright red rose hips that attract countless birds. Pollinators visit during the growing season.

Winterberry

Ilex verticillata • Zones 3 to 9
Few deciduous shrubs garner as much cold-weather interest as winterberry. Unlike most of its holly cousins, it drops its leaves in the autumn, so nothing detracts from the brilliance of the red berries. You'll love the colorful fruit, and the birds will love you *for* it. In warmer weather, watch for Henry's elfins: This is a host plant for these little butterflies.

Witch Hazel

American Bittersweet

Celastrus scandens • Zones 3 to 8
Bittersweet's showy orange berries are a favorite of more than a dozen bird species. Growing up to 30 feet tall, it offers ample shelter. Choose it over its invasive cousin, Oriental bittersweet (*C. orbiculatus*).

American Bittersweet

Witch Hazel

Hamamelis x *intermedia* • Zones 5 to 9
Just when you're convinced that winter will never end, witch hazel explodes with masses of fragrant ribbon-petal flowers in copper, yellow or red. Depending on the cultivar and location, this deciduous shrub may blossom as early as January and hold onto its blooms until March. Later on, birds forage for the fallen seeds. The gray-green leaves turn yellow-orange with frost.

our readers share

What plants in your yard attract birds in cold weather?

"Birds like my cedar, holly and crabapple trees. Cardinals love to sit in my crabapple tree and fly in to get their feed a few feet away. They use the cedar for coverage at night."
—EMMA M., *Ward, AR*

"We have a Seckel pear tree in our backyard. Cardinals perch there along with nuthatches, woodpeckers, blue jays, juncos and a cute little Carolina wren. They leave their nests in the nearby pine and 'go outside' to hang out in the pear tree!"
—PEGGY S., *Pittsburgh, PA*

"The goldfinches really dig black-eyed Susans, coneflowers and sunflowers."
—JOE B., *South Bend, IN*

"For the juncos and chicka-deedeedees, I let the millet seeds grow that birds throw out of my feeders. We also have a beech tree that the grouse eat from regularly in the hard New York months."
—LINDA L., *via Facebook*

"I've seen hummingbirds pull the silky seed heads off my Japanese anemones in late winter and early spring, so I always leave those up. I have lots of finches and hummers year-round in Washington."
—DAWN H., *via Facebook*

"All our winter birds love the hemlock, fir and magnolia trees because they block the cold wind."
—BETSY B., *Belvidere, TN*

"I, too, leave all seed heads till spring, but the birds' favorite is the redbud tree. That's where I hang the feeders so I can watch them through the window!"
—PAULA D., *Raymore, MO*

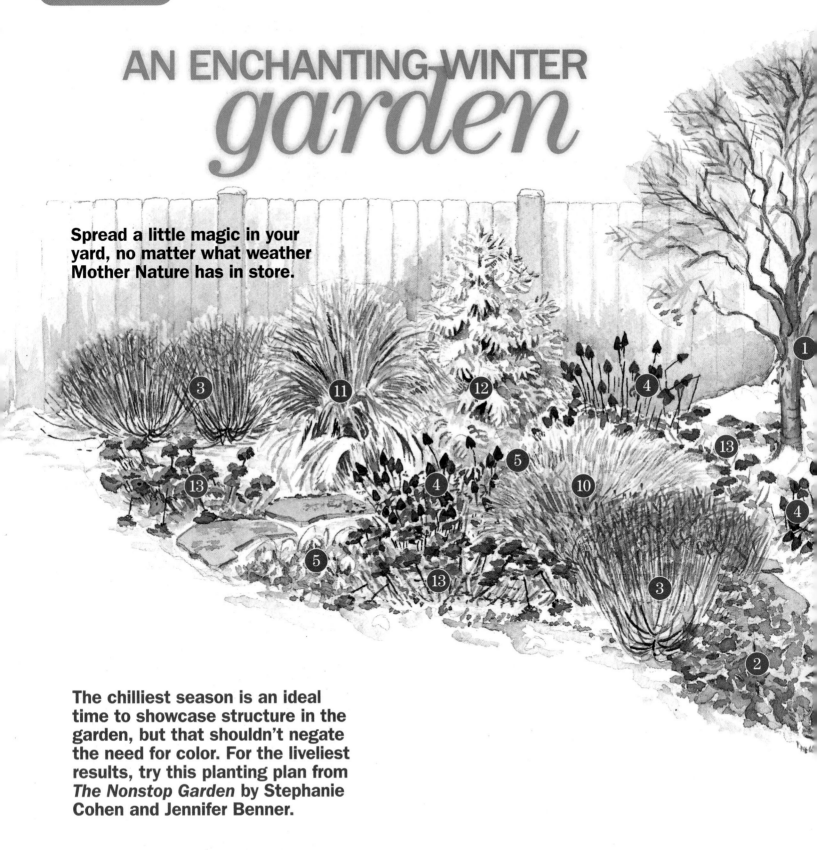

AN ENCHANTING WINTER
garden

Spread a little magic in your yard, no matter what weather Mother Nature has in store.

The chilliest season is an ideal time to showcase structure in the garden, but that shouldn't negate the need for color. For the liveliest results, try this planting plan from *The Nonstop Garden* **by Stephanie Cohen and Jennifer Benner.**

IDEAL EVERGREENS.
Conifers, such as the Colorado spruce, offer food and shelter to birds, including white-winged crossbills.

Why two winterberry cultivars? **If you want berries,** you'll need both a male and a female plant.

*Total size:
24 × 33 feet*

Winter Infusion

Perk up a drab corner of your backyard with a cold-weather refuge for birds.

1. **Paperbark maple** *Acer griseum* x *A. nikoense* 'Gingerbread,' Zones 4 to 8 ~ 1 plant

2. **False cypress** *Chamaecyparis obtusa* 'Dainty Doll,' Zones 4 to 8 ~ 1 plant

3. **Redosier dogwood** *Cornus sericea* 'Baileyi,' Zones 3 to 8 ~ 3 plants

4. **Coneflower** *Echinacea purpurea* 'Fragrant Angel,' Zones 4 to 9 ~ 15 plants

5. **Giant snowdrop** *Galanthus elwesii*, Zones 3 to 8 12 plants

6. **Witch hazel** *Hamamelis* x *intermedia* 'Jelena,' Zones 5 to 8 ~ 1 plant

7. **Hellebore** *Helleborus* 'Ivory Prince,' Zones 4 to 8 5 plants

8. **Winterberry** *Ilex verticillata* 'Jim Dandy,' Zones 3 to 9 ~ 2 plants

9. **Winterberry** *Ilex verticillata* 'Winter Red,' Zones 3 to 9 ~ 1 plant

10. **Maiden grass** *Miscanthus sinensis* 'Morning Light,' Zones 5 to 9 ~ 1 plant

11. **Bitter switchgrass** *Panicum amarum* 'Dewey Blue,' Zones 2 to 9 ~ 3 plants

12. **Colorado blue spruce** *Picea pungens* 'Baby Blueeyes,' Zones 3 to 7 ~ 1 plant

13. **Sedum** *Sedum* 'Matrona,' Zones 3 to 8 ~ 6 plants

DAZZLING WINTER
containers

Provide food and shelter to visiting birds with these chic seasonal planters.

If you're creating an all-branch combo, **use floral foam instead of soil.** It won't expand in the cold and damage the planter.

Christmas Cheer

Twisted Harry Lauder's walking stick is the perfect asymmetrical addition to this mass of vibrant foliage and berries.

LIGHT REQUIREMENTS: Any

POT SIZE: 16 inches

INGREDIENTS:

A. Harry Lauder's walking stick
1 branch

B. Heavenly bamboo with leaves and berries ~ 3 branches

C. Creeping juniper ~ 1 bough

D. Scotch broom ~ 2 boughs

E. Golden juniper ~ 2 boughs

Make
suet balls
for birds and
serve them up
on dowels!

Frosty Morning

A potted eastern arborvitae gets a makeover
in this whimsical green-and-white combination.

LIGHT REQUIREMENTS: Part to full sun

POT SIZE: 24 inches

INGREDIENTS:

A. Juniper ~ 2 boughs

B. Eastern arborvitae ~ 1 plant

C. Dried artemisia ~ 1 branch

D. Colorado blue spruce ~ 2 boughs

Extras: Faux olive branches

White-painted twigs

Warm Welcome

A feast for the eyes *and* for songbirds, this arrangement is
dotted with faux winter fruit held in place by small dowels.

LIGHT REQUIREMENTS: Any

POT SIZE: 18 inches

INGREDIENTS:

A. Golden juniper ~ 3 boughs

B. Incense-cedar ~ 3 boughs

C. Yellow holly ~ 2 branches

D. Holger juniper ~ 2 boughs

Extras: Faux kumquats

Faux apples

Yellow-twig dogwood branches

winter BIRDING *basics*

WHO'S THERE?
Look for these winter regulars.

THE DIEHARDS: A surprising number of birds stick around through the coldest months. Tree-clinging seedeaters like chickadees, nuthatches and titmice are frequent backyard visitors, especially if you have a lot of trees, and suet-eating woodpeckers tip-tap their way through the coldest days. Other year-round regulars include vibrant red cardinals and brilliant blue jays.

THE SNOWBIRDS: Juncos are often called snowbirds because they spend the year's warmest months in Canada and Alaska, but they winter throughout the United States. (Imagine flying south to Minnesota for the winter!) Look for small flocks of juncos eating on the ground beneath your seed feeders this winter.

THE IRRUPTERS: If you've ever had a flock of evening grosbeaks, pine siskins or red crossbills descend upon your winter feeding station and clean out your sunflower seed, then you know something about cold-season bird irruptions. Usually a shortage of natural food drives flocks of birds southward from their normal habitats into areas where they are not usually found.

WINTER WOW: If you're lucky enough to have a wave of crossbills fly into your backyard this winter, you'll notice something quite unusual. These birds' bills are actually crossed at the tip, allowing them to pry open and pull seeds from certain types of pinecones, their favorite food.

WHAT'S ON THE MENU?
Help birds brave the cold.

FATTY FAVES: High-fat, high-calorie foods are especially important for birds during the year's coldest months. Birds have fewer daylight hours to find food but need more calories to get through the cold nights. Add suet nuggets to your seed mix, or smear spreadable suet, called bark butter, onto a tree to give birds an extra boost.

In winter, **Carolina wrens eat seeds and suet.** They forage for bugs when it's warm.

When cold weather rolls in, so do some birds! Here's what you should know now. BY ANNE SCHMAUSS

NUT LOVERS: Peanuts in the shell are particular favorites of blue jays, which can easily crack open the shell. Watch for these picky jays to thoroughly inspect several peanuts before choosing just the right one. Birds such as black-capped chickadees and tufted titmice love the shelled variety that's found in many seed mixes.

BIRD BLOCK: Seed blocks and cylinders packed with a variety of birds' favorites offer a long-lasting, steady source of nutrition even if you don't have time to fill your feeders or if a snowstorm makes it too hard to get outside. Be sure your seed block is heavy on high-fat sunflower and nuts.

THE WINTER BASICS: A good seed mix loaded with sunflower will satisfy most seedeaters. Hang several suet feeders during the winter. Make them more stable and bird-friendly by nestling them against a tree trunk or branch. Don't be afraid to place a suet feeder right outside a window for good views—your woodpeckers won't mind.

IN A NUTSHELL
Pressed for time? Follow these quick and handy tips.

THINK AHEAD: Fill feeders and birdbaths in the midafternoon before the birds start settling in to sleep, so they are well prepared to survive the long, cold night to come.

EASIER PICKIN'S: Birds are most vulnerable after a snow or ice storm. Brush snow and ice off your feeders and your flowers so birds can harvest the leftover seeds. You might want to use part of your cleared driveway or patio for ground feeding so juncos can easily find their millet.

WATER: A clean bird is a warm bird. Clean feathers insulate birds better against the cold. Use an electric heater to keep your birdbath warm so birds can stay clean and get a drink during the cold days of winter. If temperatures dipped below freezing the previous night, add some warm water to your birdbath in the morning.

A FEATHERED FRENZY. Many birders love winter because their favorite subjects are most visible. They look forward to visits from white-breasted nuthatches (far left), pileated woodpeckers (left), dark-eyed juncos (center), blue jays (top left), red crossbills (above) and Carolina wrens (top).

Mourning Cloak

YEAR-ROUND
butterflies:
WINTER

Find out what butterflies are up to at the chilliest time of the year. BY KENN KAUFMAN

There are a few regions of North America where winter's effects are scarcely felt, and there, butterfly-watching may be exciting all year. But away from subtropical zones, winter marks the low ebb for butterfly activity.

Time to Recharge

Along the Gulf of Mexico, in the lowlands of the desert Southwest and on California's coast, mild winters allow some butterflies to keep flying. They may be out of sight on cool, cloudy days, but red admirals, painted ladies and others take wing in the warmth, no matter what the calendar says.

East of the Rockies, most monarch butterflies are absent, having flown to their wintering site in the Mexican mountains. But much of the Western population spends the season along the California coast. They are sedentary, hanging in dense clusters in their tall roosting trees. At times, though, especially on the warmest days, they will scatter to the wind like orange confetti, drifting back to the roost as evening nears.

Surviving the Cold

The monarch migration is unique: No other butterfly has such a precise migratory pattern. In fact, relatively few migrate at all. So when we don't see butterflies during the winter, they're not necessarily gone, merely out of sight. They may survive the coldest months in any of their four major life stages: egg, caterpillar (larva), pupa (chrysalis) or adult.

A few tough butterflies hibernate as adults, sleeping in sheltered crevices. A February thaw may wake them, leading to the startling sight of a mourning cloak, comma or tortoiseshell flying over snowdrifts. And a few, such as some swallowtails, spend the winter as pupae, ready to emerge as adults in spring. Others overwinter in the egg stage.

Caterpillars might seem more vulnerable, but the majority of our butterflies spend the winter in that form. They may even hatch out of the egg in fall and not begin to eat until spring. So even in the Northern midwinter, when the land is locked in ice and snow, next summer's butterflies take the shape of myriad tiny caterpillars sleeping in the cold.

GLAD YOU ASKED

Our bird and butterfly experts answer birders' most pressing winter questions.

We get robins in winter. Since the ground is frozen solid and **they have no chance of getting worms,** even though I see them try, I'm wondering what I can feed them. What else do they eat?

—HOWARD S., *Big Stone Gap, VA*

GEORGE HARRISON: Some American robins now overwinter in northern regions where they must find food in harsh, snowy weather. Though they feed heavily on tree berries and other fruit, we can supplement their diets with raisins, chopped apples and live mealworms like those we feed bluebirds. You can find worms in pet shops. The birds will feed on the ground and in tray feeders up to 6 feet off the ground.

MANY HAPPY RETURNS

Is Pacific Grove, California, the only place that **hosts overwintering butterflies**? Where else can you find butterflies in winter, aside from butterfly houses? And when do monarchs return from their wintering grounds?

—SUE S., *Farmington, MN*

TOM ALLEN: There are about 25 sites along the California coastline where monarchs from the regions west of the Rocky Mountains gather for the winter months. Those populations east of the Rockies fly south, many crossing the Gulf of Mexico into the Sierra-Madres of Central Mexico. With this migration, some fly more than 3,000 miles. In Mexico, monarchs gather by the millions to winter in roughly 12 7-1/2-acre locations.

In early March, monarchs begin their migration north. Once they cross back into the United States, they will mate and begin to lay their eggs. It is the offspring of these butterflies that will repopulate the northern habitats.

Most migratory butterflies move north in spring. These species build their populations in the South and the move north with the advancing spring temperatures.

BRING IN THE QUAIL

As "snowbirds," we spend about half the year in semirural Arizona. There are **wild quail** in the area, and we would like to attract them to our yard. We know that some people make their own quail blocks. What do you recommend?

—DUANE & CHARLOTTE T., *Renton, WA*

GEORGE: There are three backyard attractions for quail (like those in this photo sent in by reader Michael R. Duncan of Bakersfield, California). One is a dusting spot. Quail love to dust their feathers in a small area of powdered dust. You can easily create this by removing the vegetation in a small area of your yard and raking the soil.

Next, you can always draw quail in with a water hole. Think of it as a ground level birdbath. Simply line the water area with gravel, and then set up a garden hose to slowly drip into the depression.

The last thing to do is use quail-attracting food. I don't recommend making your own quail blocks because those often attract other, less desirable animals. Spread finely cracked corn on the ground near the dusting bed and water area. If you follow this advice, the quail should soon come to gather in the area several times a day.

TRUE REDHEAD

We live on a farm and love all the wildlife surrounding us. Recently **we've been watching this new visitor. Can you tell me more about this bird?**

—JUDY G., *Newton, IA*

GEORGE: The bird in your photograph is a juvenile red-headed woodpecker. From the time they leave the nesting cavity until the following February, juvenile redheads have brown heads. After that, both males and females molt into true redheads for the remainder of their lives.

ADDED INSULATION

Are there advantages to adding wood shavings or cedar sawdust to **the bottom of nest boxes** in winter?

—DICK M., *St. Peter, MN*

GEORGE: It is a good idea to add wood chips to a birdhouse in winter. Many birds use houses for roosting during the cooler months, so it helps to add some insulation for them. In turn, doing this might help attract more cavity-roosting birds at night.

Bluebirds, for instance, are one type you're likely to attract. In fact, you could even attract several bluebirds to a single birdhouse. Birds often seek warmth and insulation from each other during cold weather. I've seen pictures of as many as 13 eastern bluebirds nestled in the same house on a winter night.

So if you can, give the birds a little extra insulation this winter. You might attract a new feathered friend.

WINTER BLOOMERS

It's not unusual for us to have Anna's hummingbirds stay all year long. Are there any **winter plants that hummingbirds enjoy**?

—DIANA S., *Bellevue, WA*

GEORGE: Outside the West Coast, Gulf Coast and Southwest, most Americans see no hummingbirds in winter. The winter plants that produce nectar and attract insects for hummingbirds vary by region. In your area, bush-penstemons, pitcher sage, fuchsia-flowered gooseberry and orange bush monkey flower (shown here) are favorites.

About 30 bird species in each region of the U.S. are so-called cavity nesters, including **chickadees, tree swallows, purple martins and house wrens**. Most of them will also use a birdhouse.

^ MOOSE "HOOSE" Instead of gifts, Mellissa Pfohl Smith and her husband exchange homemade holiday cards with his sister and brother-in-law. "The 'cards' get more creative each year," says the Peekskill, New York, native. "Last year, we made this birdhouse to honor the moose that pass through their Vermont backyard."

^ WINTER CHALET "My husband, Jay, made this birdhouse from old weathered wood," writes Darlene Julian of Yerington, Nevada. "He has made dozens of birdhouses, but I think this one with the wreath and snow-covered shingled roof is one of the cutest."

BACKYARD BUILDERS

Put your backyard wildlife in the holiday spirit with these "cool" projects shared by *Birds & Blooms* fans.

< FESTIVE FEEDER Laurie Shirley of Vancouver, Washington, hosts Anna's hummingbirds all year. "We wanted to keep them warm and fed during the winter," she says. Christmas lights in an upside-down squirrel baffle keep the nectar from freezing. "Whenever we walk by the feeder, we notice a little hummer hanging out in the windy, wintry weather."

< SNOWMAN SERVES SUPPER "We found some antique pie tins at an Amish sale and turned them into bird feeders," says Sue Peterson of Newville, Pennsylvania. "My husband, Pete, cut and sanded the snowmen, and I decorated them. Then we assembled the feeders and gave them away to family and friends."

< STOCKING UP "In the spirit of the season, I decided the birds needed a holiday stocking as well," says Jeanette McDonald from Freedom, Pennsylvania. She filled a small stocking with a sprig of millet and hung it on a birdhouse. It was quite a hit with the birds!

plantable GIFT TAGS

Recycle your junk mail and encourage green thumbs with this easy project.

Cut tags in **any shape you like**! Use cookie cutters or even scissors.

For Mary

Here's a crafty way to go green and *grow* green.

ISN'T IT ABOUT TIME YOUR JUNK MAIL HAD A PURPOSE? Now you can turn it into plantable gift tags using this simple method from Kendra Zvonik. She sells these tags at her Etsy store, *greenpost.etsy.com*, using 100-percent recycled materials.

TO MAKE THE PAPER

1. Using a shredder, process paper—sorted by color, if you'd like (**fig. a**)—in batches, then soak pieces in a bucket of water for about 24 hours.

2. Remove the wet paper shreds and blend with a hand mixer, making a creamy, smooth pulp. If it's too dry, add a bit of water. Spread the mixture out to dry if you're not using it immediately.

3. When you're ready to make paper, add 1/3 pound of dried pulp to 5 gallons of clean water in a plastic tub. (If the pulp is wet, use more than 1/3 pound.) The mixture should be loose, not too watery and not too thick (like a creamy soup). Mix often to keep pulp evenly dispersed in the water.

4. Quickly but gently, submerge the mold and deckle in the tub. Immerse the front edge first, scooping the pulp away from you. If you plunge too deeply into the tub, the pulp will be too thick. If you don't go deep enough, it will be uneven or have holes in it. This takes practice, so be patient.

5. Drain any water in the mold back into the tub. Carefully pull the deckle upward and away from the mold and set aside.

6. Place your newly formed paper on a felt sheet (**fig. b**). You can achieve this by using a continuous rocking motion from the back edge of the mold to the front edge. Repeat as desired to make more sheets. Set the mold aside.

a

b

c

TO MAKE THE GIFT TAGS

1. While your newly formed sheet of paper is still wet on the felt, firmly press a cookie cutter into the pulp and then spread approximately 1/8 teaspoon of seeds inside the shape (**fig. c**).

2. Fill your squeeze bottle with pulp mixture from the tub. Using the bottle, fill the inside of the cookie cutter about halfway, covering the seeds. Let the pulp settle.

3. Remove cookie cutter. Cover the entire paper sheet with a felt sheet and sponge away the excess water.

4. Carefully flip the felt and sponge water off the back. Remove the top felt sheet. Pick up the bottom felt sheet with your paper on top and gently flip it onto a drying rack so tags are facing upward.

5. Peel and remove the felt so the paper can finish air-drying overnight.

6. Once it's dry, you can cut the shapes out, punch the holes and string them up. Use these as gift tags, rustic ornaments or party favors—be creative!

WHAT YOU NEED TO MAKE THE PAPER

Junk mail (for this project, do not use newspapers or glossy paper, like magazines)

Paper shredder

Bucket

Hand mixer

8-1/2 x 11-inch mold and deckle (make your own or buy one at *carriagehousepaper.com*)

Large plastic tub

Large sponges

Felt sheets, about 10 x 13 inches

WHAT YOU NEED TO MAKE THE GIFT TAGS

Cookie cutters

Plant seeds

Plastic squeeze bottle

Large sponge

Felt sheet

Flat clothes-drying rack

Hole punch

String

PSST! Need a shortcut? Place cookie cutters directly onto the felt sheets. Instead of using a mold and deckle to make sheets of paper, use your squeeze bottle to create the layers of pulp.

Birdseed Ornaments

Log Feeder

A FEAST
for the birds

Treat your feathered friends to a festive wintertime snack.

ACROSS NORTH AMERICA, folks are brightening their landscapes with wreaths and Christmas lights. Why not go a step further and string up some goodies for the birds?

WHAT YOU NEED TO MAKE BIRDSEED ORNAMENTS

1/3 cup unflavored gelatin

1-1/2 cups water

8 cups birdseed

Cookie cutters

Baking rack

Wire

Decorative accessories (optional)

WHAT YOU NEED TO MAKE A LOG FEEDER

Log

Drill

Large drill bit

Screw eye

Wire or sturdy string

Peanut butter

TO MAKE BIRDSEED ORNAMENTS

1. Mix gelatin and water over low heat until gelatin is melted and clear.

2. Remove from heat and stir in birdseed until it is well mixed and all the seed is moist.

3. Fill cookie cutters with the seed mixture, packing tightly. Refrigerate for 2 to 4 hours. Dry on a baking rack for 3 days.

4. Wrap a wire around each of the ornaments and form a hook at the end. Add any other embellishments you desire.

5. Display the ornaments outdoors.

TO MAKE A LOG FEEDER

1. Drill a few holes in a log, taking care not to drill all the way through or hit another hole. Attach the screw eye to the top of the log and tie on a sturdy wire or string for hanging.

2. Fill the holes with peanut butter and hang the log where you—and the birds—can see it!

FEEDER
from a frame

Turn a picture frame that's seen better days into a delightful bird feeder. BY **ALISON AUTH**

OLD PICTURE FRAMES MAKE PERFECT FEEDERS. With a few supplies and these simple instructions, make an inexpensive but lovely tray feeder for winter birds.

1. Paint your picture frame, if desired.

2. Cut the screen to fit your picture frame opening and staple it to the back.

3. Using either a hammer and a finishing nail or a drill bit, make pilot holes in the four corners of the finished side of the frame for your screw eyes. Twist them in.

4. Cut four equal lengths of chain or wire and attach one to each screw eye.

5. Gather at the top and run the shower curtain hanger through the ends of the chain or loops in the wire. Hang filled feeder from the nearest branch!

WHAT YOU NEED

Old picture frame

Paint and brush (optional)

Window screen

Snips or scissors for cutting screen

Stapler and staples

Hammer and finishing nail or drill bit and drill for pilot holes

4 screw eyes

Chain or wire

Wire cutters (if using stiff chain or wire)

Shower curtain hanger or something similar for gathering the chain or wire

Reader Lori Anderson of Gwynn, Michigan, tells us that **after seeing the project in *Birds & Blooms***, her husband, Jerry, was inspired to make this feeder!

Barred Owl
Brenda Foubert ~ Seeleys Bay, ON

Frosted Berry
Lee Wendland ~ Willis, MI

Pine Grosbeak
Sandra Bertin Ross ~ Kaministiquia, ON

Red-Bellied Woodpecker
Tom King ~ Elizabethtown, KY

Northern Cardinal
Lori Tambakis ~ Washington,

WINTER GARDEN
gallery

Feast your eyes on these quintessential
wintertime sights, captured through
the lenses of *Birds & Blooms* readers.

Bluebird Family
Don Scott ~ Goodlettsville, TN

Icicle
Kathy Fritzges ~ Dallas, PA

Northern Cardinal
Jeanne Koch ~ Harlan, IA

Winter Heath
Sue Rager ~ Murphy, NC

attention, shutterbugs!
Want to see your
snapshots featured
in *Birds & Blooms*
publications?
Submit them to
birdsandblooms.com
or mail them in!

Carolina Wren
Linda Bumpus ~ Cunningham, TN

north american BIRDS

Get to know the birds in your own backyard.

Now that you've learned all the tools to welcoming birds to your space, all that's missing are the tricks to identifying your winged visitors. This section gives you a good head start, with 69 birds that are commonly seen in yards, forests, fields and wetlands across the U.S. and Canada.

key

- winter
- summer
- year-round
- migration

bluebirds

Fifty years ago, the return of bluebirds—especially eastern bluebirds—to northern states in March signaled the arrival of warmer weather. But with mild winters becoming more common during the past decades, many bluebirds now spend winters in their nesting areas all across the North.

A week or two after the male arrives, the female appears. Then, to the accompaniment of his own incessant warbling, the male pursues his chosen mate from one perch to another, often showing her spots available for nesting.

Making a Comeback

In the early to mid-1900s, bluebirds almost became extinct. But today, all three species—eastern, western and mountain—are at healthy population levels, and the future looks bright.

They still face challenges, however, such as competition for nesting sites from house sparrows, house wrens, European starlings and tree swallows. Often, just about the time a pair of bluebirds begins to nest, one of the four enemy birds takes over.

House wrens will even poke holes in the bluebirds' eggs. What's especially frustrating about this aggressive behavior is that once they win the battle, these other birds often vacate the house.

Nesting starts early among bluebirds, so they can raise at least two broods each year. It's common for the first brood to help their parents feed the second brood, a practice known as "cooperative breeding." As the song says, these lovely and popular birds are truly the "bluebird of happiness," bringing excitement, color and adventure to any backyard. —*George Harrison*

Backyard Bio

Common Names: Eastern, western and mountain bluebird.

Scientific Names: *Sialia sialis*, *S. mexicana* and *S. currucoides*, respectively.

Length: 7 inches.

Wingspan: 13 to 14 inches.

Distinctive Markings: Males generally have a blue back, wings and head, with a white belly, except for the mountain bluebird, which is brilliant blue all over. Orange on the breast extends onto the throat. Females generally have the same markings, but duller, except for western females, which are gray overall with pale-blue feathers on tail and wings.

Voice: Soft "tru-al-ly, tru-al-ly" warble for eastern; mountain is similar but higher pitched; and western's is a subdued "f-few, f-few, f-few."

Habitat: Open backyards and farmland.

Nesting: Built mostly by the female, the nest is made of dried grasses and lined with finer grasses, hair and feathers. She lays four to six pale-blue eggs between March and July for eastern, April and May for western and April and July for mountain.

Diet: Insects and berries.

Backyard Favorite: Live mealworms.

Eastern Bluebird

Western Bluebird

Mountain Bluebird

Pine Grosbeak

Evening Grosbeak

Rose-Breasted Grosbeak

Black-Headed Grosbeak

A member of the finch family, **the cold-loving pine grosbeak can be found in parts of North America, Europe and Asia**. True to its name, this songbird is attracted to pinecones.

Pine Grosbeak
Scientific Name: *Pinicola enucleator*.
Length: 9 inches.
Wingspan: 14 inches.
Distinctive Markings: The males are red with gray. Females are grayish with yellow on their heads.
Voice: A short, clear and musical warble.
Habitat: Open areas and edges of coniferous forests, along streams or ponds and in wooded suburbs.
Nesting: Bulky, loose nest of twigs and roots. Female lays three to five blue-green speckled eggs.
Diet: Tree seeds, berries and some insects.
Backyard Favorite: Sunflower seeds.

Evening Grosbeak
Scientific Name: *Coccothraustes vespertinus*.
Length: 8 inches.
Wingspan: 14 inches.
Distinctive Markings: Males are yellow and brownish with a black tail, white wing patches and a yellow band above their eyes. Females are grayish with similar marks.
Voice: Sharp, high and trilling "kleerr" call.
Habitat: Coniferous forests and western mountains.
Nesting: Shallow cup-shaped nests. Lays two to five blue or turquoise eggs.
Diet: Insects in summer; seeds and buds in winter.
Backyard Favorite: Sunflower seeds at a tray feeder.

Rose-Breasted Grosbeak
Scientific Name: *Pheucticus ludovicianus*.
Length: 8 inches.
Wingspan: 12-1/2 inches.
Distinctive Markings: Male is black and white with a rose-red triangle on his breast. Females are dark brown with white streaked underparts.
Voice: Long, continuous robinlike whistle.
Habitat: Small trees and shrubs in gardens and parks.
Nesting: Males and females build loose nests.
Diet: Forages in trees for seeds, insects and fruit.
Backyard Favorites: May come to feeders for sunflower and safflower seeds.

Black-Headed Grosbeak
Scientific Name: *Pheucticus melanocephalus*.
Length: 8-1/4 inches.
Wingspan: 12-1/2 inches.
Distinctive Markings: Males have black head, brownish-orange underparts and bicolored bill; black and white tail and white wing patches. Female is brown with stripes.
Voice: Whistled warble, faster, higher and choppier than the rose-breasted.
Habitat: Along water and open woods.
Nesting: Build in dense outer foliage of tree or shrub.
Diet: Seeds, berries and insects.
Backyard Favorites: Sunflower and safflower seeds.

American Robin

Scientific Name: *Turdus migratorius.*
Length: 10 inches.
Wingspan: 17 inches.
Distinctive Markings: Male has orange breast, black head and tail, white around eyes and on throat. Females are duller.
Voice: Loud, liquid song, "cheerily, cheer-up, cheerio."
Habitat: Yards, fields, farms and woods.
Nesting: Three to four pastel-blue eggs in a neat, deep cup made of mud and grass.
Diet: Earthworms. Also eats insects, berries and some seeds.
Backyard Favorites: Fruit, sunflower seeds and peanut butter.

Wood Thrush

Scientific Name: *Hylocichla mustelina.*
Length: 7-3/4 inches.
Wingspan: 13 inches.
Distinctive Markings: Potbellied bird with a reddish crown and neck, white eye ring and a bold black-spotted breast.
Voice: Tranquil, peaceful liquid song: "Ger-al-deeeeen."
Habitat: Wooded areas.
Nesting: Females build nest in the crotch of a tree or shrub. Resembles a robin's nest.
Diet: Insects and a wide range of fruits and berries.
Backyard Favorites: Feeders with fruit or bird cakes made with cornmeal, peanut butter and beef suet.

Mourning Dove

Scientific Name: *Zenaida macroura.*
Length: 12 inches.
Wingspan: 18 inches.
Distinctive Markings: Both are brown-gray and pigeon-like with a long, pointed tail with white edges conspicuous in flight.
Voice: "Coo-ah, cooo, cooo, coo."
Habitat: Open woods, evergreen plantations, orchards, farmlands and suburban backyards and gardens.
Nesting: Commonly found in an evergreen. Builds a loose, bulky platform of sticks in which it lays two pure-white eggs. Pairs raise two to five broods each year.
Diet: Seeds and plant materials.
Backyard Favorites: Seed mix or cracked corn.

Northern Mockingbird

Scientific Name: *Mimus polyglottos.*
Length: 10 inches.
Wingspan: 14 inches.
Distinctive Markings: Both sexes are gray with grayish-white undersides and white patches on the bottom of their wings.
Voice: Almost unlimited variations. Talented mimic. Repeats songs several times with a pause before a new series.
Habitat: Backyards, pastures, hedges and woodland edges.
Nesting: Pairs build cup-shaped nests in the fork of a shrub. Lays three to six blue or green eggs with brown splotches.
Diet: Insects, fruit and berries.
Backyard Favorites: Berries, suet and mealworms.

American Robin

Wood Thrush

Mourning Dove

Northern Mockingbird

Yellow Warbler

Common Yellowthroat

Prothonotary Warbler

Yellow-Rumped Warbler

Yellow Warbler
Scientific Name: *Dendroica petechia.*
Length: 5 inches.
Wingspan: 8 inches.
Distinctive Markings: Male is bright yellow with reddish-brown streaks on breast; female is duller yellow.
Voice: "Sweet sweet sweet sweet sweeter sweeter" or "sweet-sweet-sweet-chit-tit-tit-teweet."
Habitat: Gardens, marshes, orchards and thickets.
Nesting: Strong, compact cup of firmly interwoven hemp, grasses and plant down. Built in upright fork of shrub or tree.
Diet: Insects—mostly caterpillars.
Backyard Favorite: Birdbaths, especially with moving water.

Common Yellowthroat
Scientific Name: *Geothlypis trichas.*
Length: 5 inches.
Wingspan: 6-3/4 inches.
Distinctive Markings: Male has a bright yellow throat and black mask across its forehead. Females lack the mask.
Voice: A gentle whistle of "wichity-wichity-wichity."
Habitat: Prairie, pine forest, wetlands.
Nesting: Bulky nest filled with dead grasses, hair and more.
Diet: Mostly insects, including grubs and caterpillars.
Backyard Favorite: Birdbaths.

Prothonotary Warbler
Scientific Name: *Protonotaria citrea.*
Length: 5-1/2 inches.
Wingspan: 8-1/2 inches.
Distinctive Markings: A bright-golden warbler with blue-gray wings and tail, with white below. Female is duller.
Voice: A series of loud, ringing sweet notes.
Habitat: Swamps, bottomlands and near water.
Nesting: Females construct nests in cavities out of mosses, rootlets, twigs and leaves; four to six creamy, spotted eggs.
Diet: Mostly aquatic insects, plus some mollusks.
Backyard Favorites: Birdbaths.

Yellow-Rumped Warbler
Scientific Name: *Dendroica coronata.*
Length: 5-1/2 inches.
Wingspan: 9-1/4 inches.
Distinctive Markings: Grayish males have a yellow crown. Females are brownish. Both have bright-yellow patches on their rump and flanks, best seen in flight.
Voice: High-pitched "swee swee swee swee swee."
Habitat: Woodlands, mountains, scrub and open areas.
Nesting: A neat, deep cup on a horizontal conifer branch.
Diet: Insects in summer, and berries in winter.
Backyard Favorites: During nesting season, birdbaths. In winter, they will eat bird cakes.

Screech Owl

Great Horned Owl

Horned Lark

Meadowlark

Eastern and Western Screech Owl

Scientific Names: *Otus asio* and *O. kennicottii.*
Length: 8-1/2 inches.
Wingspan: 20 inches.
Distinctive Markings: Gray, red or brown with heavy streaks below and darker bars on back; small ear-like tufts on head. The western's bill is slightly darker.
Voice: A tremulous cry or whinny.
Habitat: Deciduous trees and near waterways.
Nesting: In a natural cavity or large birdhouse, the female lays four to five white eggs.
Diet: Insects, mammals, birds, fish, spiders and reptiles.
Backyard Favorite: A large birdhouse in which to roost and nest.

Great Horned Owl

Scientific Name: *Bubo virginianus.*
Length: 18 to 25 inches.
Wingspan: 3 to 5 feet.
Distinctive Markings: Large ear tufts; regional coloring.
Voice: "Whoo! Whoo-whoo-whoo! Whoo! Whoo!" Female call is higher pitched.
Habitat: Wooded areas, including parklands in suburban and urban sites.
Nesting: Hollow trunks where female lays one to three eggs in late winter. Also inhabits man-made platforms.
Diet: Primarily mice, rats and rabbits, but also small mammals, birds, insects, reptiles and amphibians.
Backyard Favorites: Large trees for roosting and hollow or broken trunks for nesting.

Horned Lark

Scientific Name: *Eremophila alpestris.*
Length: 7-1/4 inches.
Wingspan: 12 inches.
Distinctive Markings: Males have a black mask and breast band surrounded by bright yellow. Females look duller. Two "horned" tufts of feathers point backward.
Voice: Song is a few lisping chips, followed by a rapid, tinkling and rising trill.
Habitat: Large, open grasslands in rural areas.
Nesting: On the ground, the female builds a shallow cup of course stems, leaves and grasses. Females incubate the three to five eggs.
Diet: Seeds and insects, usually in open fields.
Backyard Favorites: Uncommon at feeders, but they may eat seeds on the ground when food is scarce.

Eastern and Western Meadowlark

Scientific Names: *Sturnella magna* and *S. neglecta.*
Length: 9-1/2 inches.
Wingspan: 14 to 14-1/2 inches.
Distinctive Markings: Species appear identical: a black "V" from their throats to their bright-yellow breasts.
Voice: The western song starts with several whistles, followed by a jumble of sounds. The eastern's song is a simple, clear and slurred, "spring o' the year."
Habitat: Prairie-like areas.
Nesting: Three to five spotted white eggs on the ground.
Diet: Mostly insects, some grains.
Backyard Favorites: Large, unmowed lawns.

The vociferous western meadowlark is the **official bird of six U.S. states:** Kansas Nebraska, Montana, Oregon, North Dakota and Wyoming.

Ruby-Throated Hummingbird

Black-Chinned Hummingbird

Rufous Hummingbird

Anna's Hummingbird

Ruby-Throated Hummingbird
Scientific Name: *Archilochus colubris.*
Length: 3-3/4 inches.
Wingspan: 4-1/2 inches.
Distinctive Markings: Ruby-red throat on male; both sexes have metallic-green back and head.
Voice: Faint; a rapid series of chipping notes.
Habitat: Areas with plentiful nectar-rich flowers.
Nesting: Cup-shaped nest the diameter of a quarter and camouflages it with lichens. Lays two tiny, white eggs.
Diet: Nectar, insects and tree sap.
Backyard Favorites: Sugar water and bright, trumpet-shaped flowers.

Black-Chinned Hummingbird
Scientific Name: *Archilochus alexandri.*
Length: 3-3/4 inches.
Wingspan: 4-3/4 inches.
Distinctive Markings: Male has a black chin with a purple band below it. Female's throat is pale.
Voice: A high, weak warble.
Habitat: Mountainous areas from foothills to summits, gardens and areas near rivers.
Nesting: Nest is a round cup made of plant down, about 1-1/2 inches across and coated with spiders' silk, usually attached to a branch or tree fork. Females lay two white eggs.
Diet: Flower nectar, tree sap, pollen and insects.
Backyard Favorite: Sugar water.

Rufous Hummingbird
Scientific Name: *Selasphorus rufus.*
Length: 3-3/4 inches.
Wingspan: 4-1/2 inches.
Distinctive Markings: Male is reddish brown on back, head and tail; scarlet throat. Female is metallic green above, with pale, rust-colored sides.
Voice: Call note is "chewp chewp."
Habitat: Open areas and woodland edges.
Nesting: May nest in loose colonies, with up to 10 nests.
Diet: Nectar and tree sap.
Backyard Favorites: Attracted to red flowers; sugar water at feeders.

Anna's Hummingbird
Scientific Name: *Calypte anna.*
Length: 4 inches.
Wingspan: 5-1/4 inches.
Distinctive Markings: Adult males have iridescent red crown and throat. Females have red patch on throat and white markings over eyes.
Voice: Call is a high sharp "stit."
Habitat: Gardens and parks that provide nectar-producing flowers.
Nesting: Made of plant down held together with spider webs. Females lay two small white eggs.
Diet: Nectar, sugar water, spiders, small insects and tree sap.
Backyard Favorite: Sugar water.

If a dominant male bully hummingbird is scaring off others, **put up additional feeders** out of the alpha male's line of sight.

Tree Swallow

Scientific Name: *Tachycineta bicolor.*
Length: 5-3/4 inches.
Wingspan: 14-1/2 inches.
Distinctive Markings: Iridescent greenish-blue above and white below. Females may be slightly duller.
Voice: Early morning singers while in flight. Also uses quick, repetitious call of "silip" or "chi-veet."
Habitat: Open fields and woodland edges near water.
Nesting: Female builds nest of grasses and white feathers in tree cavities and bluebird boxes.
Diet: Insects, plus berries and seeds in cold weather.
Backyard Favorite: Offer white feathers for nesting material.

Purple Martin

Scientific Name: *Progne subis.*
Length: 7 to 8 inches.
Wingspan: 16 to 17 inches.
Distinctive Markings: Males are iridescent blue-black all over, while females and juveniles have light-gray breasts.
Voice: Low, rich and liquid gurgling.
Habitat: Near water and large open areas.
Nesting: Eastern birds primarily choose man-made housing. Western birds often nest in natural tree and cactus cavities.
Diet: Flying insects.
Backyard Favorite: Will eat crushed eggshells for calcium.

Chimney Swift

Scientific Name: *Chaetura pelagica.*
Length: 5-1/4 inches.
Wingspan: 14 inches.
Distinctive Markings: Both males and females are sooty gray, with short bodies and long curved wings.
Voice: Constant chattering during flight.
Habitat: Open—often urban—areas.
Nesting: Using sticks and thick glue-like saliva, they affix nests to walls. Females usually lay four to five white eggs.
Diet: Flying insects.
Backyard Favorite: Faux chimneys attract them to nest.

Whip-Poor-Will

Scientific Name: *Caprimulgus vociferus.*
Length: 9 inches.
Wingspan: 18 inches.
Distinctive Markings: Heavily mottled with gray, black and brown above and paler below. The male has white patch borders below its black throat and the tips of its outer tail feathers. Females are buff-colored in those areas.
Voice: Distinctive repeated night call: "whip-poor-will."
Habitat: Open deciduous woodlands.
Nesting: None. The female lays two light-brown spotted eggs in dead leaves on the ground.
Diet: Small flying insects caught in flight.
Backyard Favorite: Bugs.

Tree Swallow

Purple Martin

Chimney Swift

Whip-Poor-Will

House Wren

House Wren
Scientific Name: *Troglodytes aedon.*
Length: 4-3/4 inches.
Wingspan: 6 inches.
Distinctive Markings: Dark-brown above and lighter below.
Voice: The male's bubbling, chattering, repetitive song rises and then falls at the end.
Habitat: Along the edges of woodlands and yards with trees.
Nesting: Will nest in strange places—boots, car radiators and mailboxes—as well as in small birdhouses. Nest built of sticks and lined with plant fibers, feathers and rubbish.
Diet: Insects, including caterpillars.
Backyard Favorite: A small birdhouse near a tree.

Carolina Wren

Carolina Wren
Scientific Name: *Thryothorus ludovicianus.*
Length: 5-1/2 inches.
Wingspan: 7-1/2 inches.
Distinctive Markings: Rusty-brown with a white eye stripe.
Voice: Song often heard as "tea-kettle, tea-kettle, tea-kettle."
Habitat: Brush and heavy undergrowth in forests, parks, wooded suburbs and gardens.
Nesting: Builds bulky nest of grass, bark, weed stalks, feathers and other materials in tree cavities, woodpiles, sheds, flower baskets, mailboxes and more. Female incubates five to six pale-pink spotted eggs.
Diet: Spiders and insects, plus some berries and seeds.
Backyard Favorites: Peanuts, suet and peanut butter.

White-Breasted Nuthatch

White-Breasted Nuthatch
Scientific Name: *Sitta carolinensis.*
Length: 5-3/4 inches.
Wingspan: 11 inches.
Distinctive Markings: Males and females look similar, with a blue-gray back and wings, black cap and white breast.
Voice: Nasal "yank-yank-yank" call.
Habitat: Areas with plentiful trees.
Nesting: Builds in natural cavities and birdhouses. Lays five to 10 white eggs with multicolored markings.
Diet: Insects and larvae; tree nuts, seeds and berries.
Backyard Favorites: Sunflower seeds, unsalted peanuts, birdseed mix and suet.

Red-Breasted Nuthatch

Red-Breasted Nuthatch
Scientific Name: *Sitta canadensis.*
Length: 4-1/2 inches.
Wingspan: 8-1/2 inches.
Distinctive Markings: Black eye line with a white stripe directly above it, rust-colored breast; female similar.
Voice: High-pitched nasal "yenk, yenk, yenk."
Habitat: Evergreen forests, and wooded yards and parks.
Nesting: Hole or cavity in a tree or a nest box.
Diet: Insects, berries, nuts and seeds.
Backyard Favorites: Sunflower seeds and suet.

northern cardinal

Northern cardinals may be the perfect backyard bird. These birds with the jaunty crests have everything going for them: They're hardy in the winter, sing during the summer and, most of all, they love to eat at backyard feeders.

Cardinal courtship, which begins in late winter, is quite touching to observe. To please his mate, the male picks up a sunflower seed and passes it to her. The female then selects a site and builds a bulky nest at about eye level. Though the female does most of the work, the male frequently feeds her and the young after they hatch.

Northern cardinals have expanded their range, appearing farther north and west to the Rocky Mountains and into the Southwest. Though adults are not truly migratory, young birds do wander around a great deal in search of mates and territories. Most don't go far, but there are exceptions. —*George Harrison*

A male cardinal is **devoted to his mate**, aggressive toward competitors and an attentive father.

Backyard Bio

Common Name: Northern cardinal.

Scientific Name: *Cardinalis cardinalis*.

Length: 8-3/4 inches.

Wingspan: 12 inches.

Distinctive Markings: Male is bright red with a black face. Also has a prominent crest and red bill. Female is fawn colored with red accents.

Voice: Over two dozen different songs. Most common is "What cheer! What cheer! What cheer!"

Habitat: Sheltered backyards, woodland edges and parks.

Nesting: Three to four whitish-gray eggs with brown speckles. Builds a nest of twigs and grasses hidden in dense trees or shrubs.

Diet: Seeds in winter; insects, such as beetles and cicadas, in the summer; berries and other fruits when they are available.

Backyard Favorites: Sunflower seeds, safflower seeds and cracked corn.

Eastern Towhee

Spotted Towhee

Northern Flicker

Hairy Woodpecker

Notice how these two towhees look quite similar? In the past, **they were both classified as the rufous-sided towhee**. The two species do occasionally breed where their territories meet, creating hybrids.

Eastern Towhee
Scientific Name: *Pipilo erythrophthalmus.*
Length: 8-1/2 inches.
Wingspan: 10-1/2 inches.
Distinctive Markings: Black head, back and tail with a white belly, orange-red sides and red or white eyes, varies by region.
Voice: Musical with a slow song, "Drink your teeeeee."
Habitat: Pastures, woodland edges and brushy yards.
Nesting: Builds nest near the ground. Female lays three to four gray speckled eggs.
Diet: Insects, spiders, caterpillars, seeds, berries and small salamanders.
Backyard Favorites: Oats or flaxseed scattered on the ground; suet.

Spotted Towhee
Scientific Name: *Pipilo maculatus.*
Length: 8-1/2 inches.
Wingspan: 10-1/2 inches.
Distinctive Markings: Black head, back and tail with a white belly, orange-red sides and white wing marks.
Voice: Wide variety of songs, usually high-pitched introductory notes followed by a trill. Also has a buzzy, rapid trill.
Habitat: Pastures, woodland edges and brushy yards.
Nesting: Builds nest near or on the ground. Female lays three to four speckled gray eggs.
Diet: Insects, spiders, caterpillars, seeds, berries and small salamanders.
Backyard Favorites: Oats or flaxseed scattered on the ground; suet.

Northern Flicker
Scientific Name: *Colaptes auratus.*
Length: 12-1/2 inches.
Wingspan: 20 inches.
Distinctive Markings: Eastern and western males sport black and red mustaches, respectively. Females don't have the mustache. For eastern birds, the wings and tail include yellow feathers; these are red in western birds.
Voice: "Flicka, flicka" or loud "wick, wick, klee."
Habitat: Backyards, orchards and open woodlands.
Nesting: Males and females excavate nesting cavities in dead trees, utility poles and fence posts. Females lay six to eight white eggs, and males incubate them at night.
Diet: Insects, fruits, berries and weed seeds.
Backyard Favorite: Large birdhouse at least 10 feet above the ground.

Hairy Woodpecker
Scientific Name: *Picoides villosus.*
Length: 9-1/4 inches.
Wingspan: 15 inches.
Distinctive Markings: Black-and-white checked back, with long, heavy bill and inconspicuous tuft. Females similar to males, but lack red mark on back of head.
Voice: Strong "peek" or "peech."
Habitat: Deciduous forests.
Nesting: Pair excavates cavity. Females usually lay four white eggs.
Diet: Insects, larvae of woodborers, fruit and nuts.
Backyard Favorites: Suet, sunflower seeds, meat scraps and peanut butter.

Red-Headed Woodpecker

Red-Bellied Woodpecker

Downy Woodpecker

Pileated Woodpecker

Red-Headed Woodpecker

Scientific Name: *Melanerpes erythrocephalus.*
Length: 9-1/4 inches.
Wingspan: 17 inches.
Distinctive Markings: Red feathers completely cover head and neck. Male and female look the same.
Voice: Harsh "queeah, queeah, queeah."
Habitat: Open woodlands.
Nesting: Excavates hole in trees, posts or utility poles.
Diet: Insects, berries and nuts.
Backyard Favorites: Cracked sunflower seeds and suet.

Red-Bellied Woodpecker

Scientific Name: *Melanerpes carolinus.*
Length: 9-1/4 inches.
Wingspan: 16 inches.
Distinctive Markings: Males have a zebra-striped back, red hood and nape with a reddish tinge on bellies. Females are identical, except for red napes.
Voice: Males and females drum on trees and siding to "sing." They also have a call note that sounds like "chiv, chiv, chiv."
Habitat: Bottomland woods, swamps, coniferous and deciduous forests, and shade trees in backyards.
Nesting: Both sexes drill a nesting cavity in a tree, utility pole or wooden building. The female lays four or five pure-white eggs, which both parents incubate.
Diet: Larvae, insects, acorns and berries.
Backyard Favorites: Medium cracked sunflower seeds on a tray feeder, suet, orange halves and sugar water.

Downy Woodpecker

Scientific Name: *Picoides pubescens.*
Length: 6-3/4 inches.
Wingspan: 12 inches.
Distinctive Markings: White belly and black-and-white elsewhere; male has a small red spot on the back of its head. Resembles a small hairy woodpecker.
Voice: Both male and female "sing" in early spring by drumming on trees. Their call note is a single "tchick."
Habitat: Open deciduous woodlands.
Nesting: Pair creates a cavity in a tree. The female lays four or five pure-white eggs.
Diet: Mostly insects, but also fruit, seeds and nuts.
Backyard Favorites: Suet, bird cakes, cracked sunflower and safflower seeds.

Pileated Woodpecker

Scientific Name: *Dryocopus pileatus.*
Length: 16-1/2 inches.
Wingspan: 29 inches.
Distinctive Markings: Both sexes have a bright-red crest, but the male's extends down its forehead. The male has a red streak at the base of its bill; the female's is black.
Voice: Both sexes have a "yucka-yucka-yucka" call.
Habitat: Woodlands, swamps and wooded backyards.
Nesting: Pairs excavate cavities in trees, often near water, for nesting. Females lay three or four white eggs on a bed of wood chips.
Diet: Insects, nuts, fruits and seeds.
Backyard Favorites: Suet on a mounted feeder; nuts.

It can take a pileated woodpecker **as many as 30 days** to carve out its oval-shaped nesting cavity.

orioles

Few songbirds are more visually striking—or create more excitement for birders—than orioles.

No matter where you live in the continental United States and parts of Southern Canada, you should be able to attract a brilliant oriole to your backyard. All you have to do is know what they crave (oranges and grape jelly fit the bill)—and offer some tree cover for their protection.

True, orioles have a sweet tooth. But it seems their desire for citrus wanes a bit just about the time they start feeding their youngsters insects and caterpillars at the nest. That's when it's important to have a sugar water feeder.

Colorful for Blackbirds

Even though they're one of the most brilliant backyard birds, all North American orioles belong to the blackbird family. Unlike other members, however, they spend most of their time high up in the treetops, rather than on the ground.

When orioles return to their northern breeding territories, they look for tree cover and stay well hidden in their search for food. The females also build their incredible nests high above the ground, weaving them from fibers of grasses, grapevines and milkweed.

Fab Five

Nine different orioles live throughout the continental United States during the breeding months, but the most common are the Baltimore, Bullock's, orchard, hooded and Scott's. Four others—the altimera, Audubon's, spot-breasted and streak-backed—are rarely spotted or occupy very small territories along the southernmost borders of the United States.

But no matter what the species is, if you cover the basics—trees, fruit and sugar water—there's a good chance a flashy oriole will visit your backyard in spring. —*Jeff Nowak*

Baltimore Oriole

Bullock's Oriole

Orchard Oriole

Backyard Bio

Common Names: Baltimore, Bullock's and orchard oriole.

Scientific Names: *Icterus galbuba, I. bullockii* and *I. spurious,* respectively.

Length: 7-1/4 to 9 inches.

Wingspan: 9-1/2 to 12 inches.

Distinctive Markings: Male Baltimore has full black hood, Bullock's has black crown with orange cheeks and white wing patches and orchard has black hood and chestnut feathers. The female Baltimore is drab yellow with dusky brown wings, the Bullock's is mostly yellow with gray back and the orchard is dusky yellow-green and gray.

Voice: Short series of clear whistles in a varied pattern for Baltimore, short series of nasal-like whistles for Bullock's and high, lively warble for orchard.

Habitat: Deciduous woodlands, open areas and suburbs.

Nesting: Pouch-like structure woven from plant fibers.

Diet: Beetles, bugs, caterpillars and fruit.

Backyard Favorites: Fruit slices, fruit trees or shrubs and nectar feeders.

Tufted Titmouse

Tufted Titmouse

Scientific Name: *Baeolophus bicolor.*
Length: 6-1/2 inches.
Wingspan: 9-3/4 inches.
Distinctive Markings: Gray above and white below, rusty-brown flanks, prominent pointed crest and large dark eyes.
Voice: Call sounds like "peto, peto, peto."
Habitat: Deciduous woodlands, preferably in swamps and river bottoms; residential wooded areas.
Nesting: Natural cavities in trees.
Diet: Insects, berries and seeds.
Backyard Favorites: Sunflower and safflower seeds, nuts, peanut butter and suet.

Pine Siskin

Pine Siskin

Scientific Name: *Carduelis pinus.*
Length: 5 inches.
Wingspan: 9 inches.
Distinctive Markings: Sexes appear similar, with brown-streaked bodies and touches of yellow on wings and tails. Males have more yellow plumage, visible during flight.
Voice: Ranges from a tuneful "sweeet" to a harsh "zzzzz."
Habitat: Backyards and coniferous forests.
Nesting: Females build shallow nests of twigs and grasses, lined with fur or feathers.
Diet: Seeds, nuts, vegetable shoots, rock salt and insects.
Backyard Favorites: Nyjer in a tube feeder with multiple perches. Also will eat cracked sunflower seeds.

Dark-Eyed Junco

Dark-Eyed Junco

Scientific Name: *Junco hyemalis.*
Length: 6-1/4 inches.
Wingspan: 9-1/4 inches.
Distinctive Markings: Common characteristics are dark eyes, white-edged tails and dark hoods; juncos interbreed freely.
Voice: Trills vary, from dry notes to tingling sounds.
Habitat: Near feeders, forests and bogs.
Nesting: Cup-shaped nest on ground. Lays four to six eggs.
Diet: Seeds, nuts and grains in winter; insects, berries and grass seeds in summer.
Backyard Favorites: Birdseed and cracked corn on ground.

Common Redpoll

Common Redpoll

Scientific Name: *Carduelis flammea.*
Length: 5-1/4 inches.
Wingspan: 9 inches.
Distinctive Markings: Brown-streaked feathers with red crown; adult males have rose-colored feathers on their upper breast.
Voice: Short, repeated notes. Mainly call notes and trills.
Habitat: Scrub forests, tundra, brushy pastures and thickets.
Nesting: Constructed with twigs, lined with grass, moss, feathers, rootlets and animal fur.
Diet: Tree seeds as well as grass and weed seeds; insects.
Backyard Favorites: Nyjer, millet and sunflower seeds.

Song Sparrow

White-Throated Sparrow

American Tree Sparrow

Chipping Sparrow

Song Sparrow
Scientific Name: *Melospiza melodia.*
Length: 6-1/4 inches.
Wingspan: 8-1/4 inches.
Distinctive Markings: Streaked with brown; side streaks join to form central breast spot. Grayish stripe over each eye.
Voice: Male song begins with "sweet, sweet, sweet" followed by shorter notes and a trill. Distinctive call note is "chimp."
Habitat: Low, open, weedy or brushy areas.
Nesting: Well-hidden ground or low nest. Female lays three to five eggs that are greenish-white and heavily splotched.
Diet: Small weed and grass seeds in fall and winter; insects.
Backyard Favorites: Birdbaths and ground-level tray feeders with seeds, each surrounded by thickets or brush.

White-Throated Sparrow
Scientific Name: *Zonotrichia albicollis.*
Length: 6-3/4 inches.
Wingspan: 9 inches.
Distinctive Markings: White throat, yellow patches in front of eyes and heads striped with black and white or tan.
Voice: "Old Sam Peabody, Peabody, Peabody" or "Oh, sweet Canada, Canada, Canada."
Habitat: Gardens, woodlands and clearings.
Nesting: Builds nest from fine materials on or near the ground; three to six blue to green speckled eggs.
Diet: Weed seeds, fruits, buds and insects.
Backyard Favorites: Millet, sunflower, corn and other seeds.

American Tree Sparrow
Scientific Name: *Spizella arborea.*
Length: 6-3/4 inches.
Wingspan: 9-1/2 inches.
Distinctive Markings: Brick-red cap, white stripes above the eyes, brown striped back and a black dot in the center.
Song: A sweet canary-like trill in spring in preparation for migration; winter call is a "teelwit" note.
Habitat: Fields, backyards, open woodland, marshes.
Nesting: On the ground in remote areas, they build a nest of grasses and stems lined with feathers.
Diet: Mostly weed seeds.
Backyard Favorite: Seed mix in a feeder on or near the ground.

Chipping Sparrow
Scientific Name: *Spizella passerina.*
Length: 5 to 6 inches.
Wingspan: 8 inches.
Distinctive Markings: Rust cap, a white line above the eye and a black stripe through the eye.
Voice: A long, mechanical trill.
Habitat: Backyards, gardens and forest openings.
Nesting: Nest is loosely woven; commonly in evergreen tree.
Diet: Forages for small seeds and insects.
Backyard Favorite: Small seeds.

Eastern Phoebe

Scientific Name: *Sayornis phoebe.*
Length: 7 inches.
Wingspan: 10-1/2 inches.
Distinctive Markings: Dark olive on top; slightly darker head.
Voice: Birds call their own name, repeating "fee-bee, fee-bee."
Habitat: Woodlands and forest edges.
Nesting: Shelflike projection over windows, on rafters or on bridge girders. They build a nest of weeds, grasses, plant fibers and mud. Females incubate four to five white eggs.
Diet: Almost entirely insects, usually caught in flight.
Backyard Favorite: Berries.

Eastern Phoebe

black-capped chickadee

Of all the common backyard birds, the black-capped chickadee takes the prize as the most entertaining. When these vivacious and carefree birds get together, they're full of cheerful conversation. They're also remarkably tame—one might even eat seeds right from your outstretched hand.

But don't let a chickadee's petite appearance fool you. Their ability to survive harsh, sub-zero temperatures is nothing short of amazing. They accomplish this by slowing down their heart rate, breathing and energy consumption.

The black-capped is the most common and widespread of the seven species of chickadees in North America. But all are similar in appearance and display many of the same entertaining behaviors. Just set out a tube feeder of sunflower seeds, and catch a show for yourself.

Researchers have discovered that **the spacing of "dees" in a chickadee's call** reveals the danger level nearby.

Backyard Bio

Common Name: Black-capped chickadee.
Scientific Name: *Poecile atricapilla.*
Length: 5-1/4 inches.
Wingspan: 8 inches.
Distinctive Markings: Black cap and chin, white cheeks, gray back.
Voice: "Chick-a-dee-dee-dee" is its call, which many will recognize. Its song is a "phoe-bee" tune.
Habitat: Woodlands, thickets, parks and wooded backyards.
Nesting: Six to eight white eggs with brown spots. Uses birdhouses and natural cavities to protect its nest made of plant fibers, wool, hair and moss.
Diet: Insects, berries and seeds.
Backyard Favorites: Sunflower seeds, suet and nyjer.

American Goldfinch

Purple Finch

House Finch

Gray Catbird

When it comes to goldfinches, the phrase, "where there's one, there may be more" certainly holds true. **These songbirds nearly always travel in flocks.** By winter, the groups may grow up to more than 100 birds.

American Goldfinch
Scientific Name: *Carduelis tristis.*
Length: 4-1/2 to 5-1/2 inches.
Wingspan: 9 inches.
Distinctive Markings: In spring and summer, males are bright yellow with black wings, tail and forehead. Females are a duller yellow with white wing bars. In winter, both sexes are olive brown with wing bars.
Voice: Melodic flight call, "per-chick-o-ree, per-chick-o-ree." Courtship song is a canary-like sweet song.
Habitat: Open areas such as yards, fields and groves.
Nesting: Cup-shaped nest with up to six pale-blue eggs.
Diet: Seeds and berries.
Backyard Favorite: Supply nyjer in a tube feeder with multiple ports, or in a nylon stocking.

Purple Finch
Scientific Name: *Carpodacus purpureus.*
Length: 6 inches.
Wingspan: 10 inches.
Distinctive Markings: Male has a raspberry tinge, brightest on head and rump. Tail is notched. The females and juveniles are brown-gray striped.
Voice: A "fridi ferdi frididifri fridi frr" call.
Habitat: Swamps, along streams and hillsides.
Nesting: Prefers trees in dense foliage. Female lays four to five speckled pale green-blue eggs.
Diet: Mostly a seedeater, but also feeds on weeds, grasses, berries, beetles and caterpillars.
Backyard Favorites: Sunflower seeds and millet.

House Finch
Scientific Name: *Carpodacus mexicanus.*
Length: 6 inches.
Wingspan: 9-1/2 inches.
Distinctive Markings: Males have reddish foreheads, breasts and rumps. Females and juveniles are streaked grayish brown. All have brown-streaked bellies.
Voice: A varied warble, often ending in a long "veeerrr."
Habitat: Any wooded area or backyard.
Nesting: Low in shrubs, door wreaths or hanging baskets; lays four to five spotted bluish-white eggs.
Diet: Seeds of berries and weeds.
Backyard Favorites: Nyjer, sunflower, mixed birdseed, peanuts, fruit, suet and sugar water.

Gray Catbird
Scientific Name: *Dumetella carolinensis.*
Length: 8-1/2 inches.
Wingspan: 11 inches.
Distinctive Markings: Slate-gray body with a black cap and tail and a patch of rust-red feathers under tail.
Voice: Alarm call sounds like a catlike mewing; song is a mix of notes, may mimic other songbirds.
Habitat: Dense thickets, woodland edges, overgrown fields and hedgerows.
Nesting: Builds nests in backyard shrubs or thickets near creeks or swamps. Females usually lay four glossy dark greenish-blue eggs.
Diet: Insects and berries.
Backyard Favorite: Grape jelly.

Western Scrub-Jay

Scientific Name: *Aphelocoma californica*.
Length: 11-1/2 inches.
Wingspan: 15-1/2 inches.
Distinctive Markings: Bright blue with a white belly and gray patch on back. Sexes look alike.
Voice: Hoarse rising call of "shreeeenk" or a rapid series "quay-quay-quay" or "cheek-cheek-cheek."
Habitat: Dense shrubbery in wooded parks and backyards.
Nesting: Bulky nest of twigs in a low tree or shrub.
Diet: Nuts, fruits, insects and small animals.
Backyard Favorites: Peanuts, suet, sunflower seeds and cracked corn.

Western Scrub-Jay

Blue Jay

Scientific Name: *Cyanocitta cristata*.
Length: 11 inches.
Wingspan: 16 inches.
Distinctive Markings: Blue feathers and crest with gray breast.
Voice: Harsh scream, "jaaay, jaaay, jaaay."
Habitat: Backyards, parks and woodlands.
Nesting: Well hidden and often found in the crotch of a tree 10 to 25 feet above the ground. False nest of twigs built before actual nest; four to five brown-spotted greenish eggs.
Diet: Nuts, seeds, fruits, insects and frogs.
Backyard Favorites: Suet, sunflower seeds and peanuts.

Blue Jay

Steller's Jay

Scientific Name: *Cyanocitta stelleri*.
Length: 11-1/2 inches.
Wingspan: 19 inches.
Distinctive Markings: Crest and front part of body are a sooty black. The rest of body is cobalt blue or purplish.
Voice: A harsh "shaaaaar," or rapid "shek shek shek shek."
Habitat: Evergreen forests, open areas and mountains.
Nesting: Bulky nest of large sticks held together with mud. Usually built in the fork of an evergreen.
Diet: Forages for acorns, pine seeds, fruit, insects, frogs and young of smaller birds.
Backyard Favorites: Sunflower seed and peanuts.

Steller's Jay

Red-Winged Blackbird

Scientific Name: *Agelaius phoeniceus*.
Length: 8-3/4 inches.
Wingspan: 13 inches.
Distinctive Markings: Males have glossy black bodies with red and yellow shoulder patches. Females have brown backs and heavily streaked undersides.
Voice: "Kong-la-ree" or "o-ka-lee."
Habitat: Fields, marshes and near water.
Nesting: Well-camouflaged grass nest among shrubs, cattails or grasses; three to five blue-green eggs with dark scrawls.
Diet: Grains, wild seeds, insects and berries.
Backyard Favorite: Birdseed mixes.

Red-Winged Blackbird

Scarlet Tanager

Western Tanager

Scarlet Tanager

Scientific Name: *Piranga olivacea*.
Length: 7 inches.
Wingspan: 11-1/2 inches.
Distinctive Markings: Males are warm red with black wings until fall, molting to yellow-green over winter. Females look identical to yellow-green males, but with black wings and tails.
Voice: Five phrases in a rapid pattern.
Habitat: In treetops in forests, parks and residential areas.
Nesting: Shallow, saucer-shaped nests.
Diet: Insects.
Backyard Favorites: Oranges, sugar water and grape jelly.

Western Tanager

Scientific Name: *Piranga ludoviciana*.
Length: 7-1/4 inches.
Wingspan: 11-1/2 inches.
Distinctive Markings: Male has bright-yellow body, black wings with prominent white bars. Head turns red in spring and summer. Female is yellow with gray back.
Voice: Similar to a robin, "Queer-it, queer. Queer-it, queer."
Habitat: Mature forests.
Nesting: Builds loose nest of twigs high in the trees. Three to five bluish-green spotted eggs.
Diet: Insects and fruit.
Backyard Favorites: Dried fruit, oranges and sugar water.

Indigo Bunting

Indigo Bunting

Scientific Name: *Passerina cyanea*.
Length: 5-1/2 inches.
Wingspan: 8 inches.
Distinctive Markings: Males are completely blue during breeding season. Females are plain brown with buff-colored streaks and a hint of blue in their wing feathers.
Voice: Rapid notes, "sweet-sweet, zee-zee, seer-seer, sip-sip."
Habitat: Overgrown fields, orchards, roadsides and thickets.
Nesting: Cup-shaped nests hidden 2 to 12 feet off the ground in weeds or shrubs. Lays three or four bluish-white eggs.
Diet: Seeds, insects, grains and berries.
Backyard Favorites: Nyjer; birdbaths.

Lazuli Bunting

Lazuli Bunting

Scientific Name: *Passerina amoena*.
Length: 5-1/2 inches.
Wingspan: 8-3/4 inches.
Distinctive Markings: Male's breeding plumage is a bright-blue head, back and tail, cinnamon chest feathers and a white belly. Tan streaks appear in winter. Females are a buff color.
Voice: A bright, rapid song that descends and then rises.
Habitat: Brush or trees near open areas.
Nesting: A cup of coarsely woven grasses in a low shrub. Female lays four pale-blue eggs.
Diet: Insects and grass seeds.
Backyard Favorites: Mixed seed or hulled sunflower.

Cedar Waxwing

Bohemian Waxwing

Red Crossbill

Ruby-Crowned Kinglet

Cedar Waxwing

Scientific Name: *Bombycilla cedrorum*.
Length: 7-1/4 inches.
Wingspan: 12 inches.
Distinctive Markings: Head crest, black eye mask, red tips on wings, yellow at end of tail and pale yellow belly. Sexes look alike.
Voice: Irregular rhythm of high "sreee" notes.
Habitat: Backyards, parks and open woodlands.
Nesting: Nests late in the season, so young can feed on emerging berries. Female lays four to five pale-gray spotted eggs.
Diet: Fruit, tree sap, flower petals and insects.
Backyard Favorites: Birdbaths, as well as berry-producing shrubs and trees.

Bohemian Waxwing

Scientific Name: *Bombycilla garrulus*.
Length: 6 to 8 inches.
Wingspan: 14 inches.
Distinctive Markings: Gray overall with a black mask, yellow-tipped tail, white and yellow edges on wings, and red waxlike markings on adult wings. Slightly larger than the cedar waxwing.
Voice: A mid-pitched rattling trill; lower than that of the cedar waxwing.
Habitat: Coniferous or birch forests.
Nesting: Four to six blue-gray spotted eggs in a nest lined with grasses and moss, usually high in a pine tree.
Diet: Fruit and insects.
Backyard Favorites: Prefers dried fruit or berries from a backyard feeder, or berry-producing trees.

Red Crossbill

Scientific Name: *Loxia curvirostra*.
Length: 5-1/2 to 6-1/2 inches.
Wingspan: 10 to 10-3/4 inches.
Distinctive Markings: Upper and lower parts of the bill twist and overlap. Males are brick red, with dark wings and a notched black tail. Females are dusky buff yellow with dark gray wings.
Voice: Courting males sing various notes and phrases.
Habitat: Coniferous forests.
Nesting: Make saucer-like nests near tips of conifer branches. Females lay three to five brown-spotted pale-blue or pale-green eggs.
Diet: Pinecones and other tree seeds.
Backyard Favorites: Sunflower and nyjer seeds.

Ruby-Crowned Kinglet

Scientific Name: *Regulus calendula*.
Length: 4-1/4 inches.
Wingspan: 7-1/2 inches.
Distinctive Markings: Olive bird overall; males have a red crest, but it doesn't always show.
Voice: A whistled chant of "sii si sisisi berr berr berr pudi pudi pudi."
Habitat: Evergreen and deciduous forests, as well as individual trees.
Nesting: A small cup-shaped nest where the female will lay 5 to 12 eggs. It is usually located high in an evergreen tree.
Diet: Insects.
Backyard Favorite: Offer water for drinking and bathing, especially during migration times.

Despite its tiny size, **the ruby-crowned kinglet lays more eggs each year** than any other North American songbird.

north american BUTTERFLIES

Meet the winged jewels that are most likely to visit your garden.

If you've ever been in the backyard and noticed a graceful—but unidentifiable—butterfly fluttering from flower to flower, you're in luck. This helpful section features more than 30 butterflies, from the giant swallowtail to the spring azure. Next time, you'll know what traits to look for and where you'll likely see these beautiful fliers, even when they're caterpillars!

Black Swallowtail

key

- winter
- summer
- year-round

Monarch

Monarchs are famous for migrating, but **these butterflies are year-round residents** of southern California, southern Florida and Hawaii.

Queen

Monarch

Scientific Name: *Danaus plexippus.*
Wingspan: 3-1/2 to 4 inches.
Distinctive Markings: Bright orange with multiple black veins. Wings are edged in black with white speckles.
Habitat: Widespread during migration, from cities to suburban gardens to rural fields and mountain pastures. When breeding (before the southward migration), they prefer open areas with plenty of milkweed plants.
Caterpillar: White with yellow and black stripes, measuring up to 2 inches long.
Host Plant: Milkweed.

Queen

Scientific Name: *Danaus gilippus.*
Wingspan: 3 to 3-3/8 inches.
Distinctive Markings: Appears similar to monarch, especially on underside of wings. Deep orangish-brown wings with black margins and thin veins. Fine white dots speckle wing edges, with larger markings on the forewings.
Habitat: Any open area where milkweed grows—meadows, fields, deserts and near waterways.
Caterpillar: Black with white bands and yellow side markings. Antennae-like filaments along back.
Host Plant: Milkweed.

Viceroy

Scientific Name: *Limenitis archippus.*
Wingspan: 2-1/2 to 3 inches.
Distinctive Markings: Similar to the monarch with rich, russet-orange color and black veins. To set them apart, the viceroy has an extra black line curving across the hind wings.
Habitat: Canals, riversides, marshes, meadows, wood edges, roadsides, lakeshores and deltas.
Caterpillar: Mottled in color with sharply defined humps and two bristles located directly behind the head.
Host Plants: Willow, poplar, aspen, cherry, apple and hawthorn trees.

Viceroy

Mourning Cloak

Adult mourning cloaks hibernate over winter. They also **slow down during summer's hottest stretches**, a state called estivation.

Hackberry Emperor

Common Buckeye

Mourning Cloak
Scientific Name: *Nymphalis antiopa*.
Wingspan: 2-7/8 to 3-3/8 inches.
Distinctive Markings: Dark maroon wings with creamy-yellow bands at wing edges and bright-blue dots.
Habitat: Near water, forest edges, open woodlands, groves, parks and backyard gardens.
Caterpillar: Black with white speckles, numerous dark spines and larger red spots. The caterpillars have been known to feed in groups.
Host Plants: Elm, willow, aspen, birch and hackberry.

Hackberry Emperor
Scientific Name: *Asterocampa celtis*.
Wingspan: 1-3/8 to 2-1/4 inches.
Distinctive Markings: Upper sides of wings range from grayish- to reddish-brown. Wings have dark tips, distinct white dots and dark spots. Undersides of wings boast yellow-outlined dark eyespots splashed with blue.
Habitat: Wherever hackberries grow, including moist woodlands, riversides, city parks and neighborhoods.
Caterpillar: 1-1/4 inches long, green with yellow and lime stripes and dots; forked horns at both ends.
Host Plants: Hackberry trees, sugarberry, dwarf hackberry.

Common Buckeye
Scientific Name: *Junonia coenia*.
Wingspan: 2 to 2-1/2 inches.
Distinctive Markings: Brown with orange bars on forewings; large yellow-rimmed black eyespots with blue or lilac centers.
Habitat: Shorelines, roadsides, railroad embankments, swamp edges, fields and meadows.
Caterpillar: Dark green to gray with orange and yellow markings, and black spines.
Host Plants: Snapdragon, plantain, figwort, stonecrop sedums and vervain.

American Lady

Scientific Name: *Vanessa virginiensis.*
Wingspan: 1-3/4 to 2-5/8 inches.
Distinctive Markings: Irregular brown, yellow and orange patterns on uppersides; forewings have a black patch, a white spot below the patch and a white bar at the wing edge. Two large blue-ringed black eyespots on hindwing undersides distinguish the American lady from the painted lady (see below), which has four small eyespots and a tiny one.
Habitat: Gardens and open areas with low vegetation, such as coastal dunes, meadows, forest edges and roadsides.
Caterpillar: Red- and white-spotted black bodies with branched black spines separated by black and green stripes.
Host Plants: Sweet everlasting, pearly everlasting, edelweiss, artemisia, ironweed and burdock.

American Lady

Painted Lady

Scientific Name: *Vanessa cardui.*
Wingspan: 2 to 2-1/2 inches.
Distinctive Markings: Salmon-orange wings on top with white and black markings; five white spots on black forewing. Underside is patterned with black, brown and gray and four small submarginal eyespots.
Habitat: Virtually anywhere, particularly in open areas.
Caterpillar: Dark in color with a yellow stripe and short white or gray spines. Measures up to 1-1/4 inches long.
Host Plants: Thistle and related plants.

Painted Lady

Red Admiral

Scientific Name: *Vanessa atalanta.*
Wingspan: 1-3/4 to 2-1/4 inches.
Distinctive Markings: Orange-red bars across center of black forewings and at base of hind wings.
Habitat: Backyards, parks, forest edges and streambeds.
Caterpillar: About 1-1/4 inches long, ranging in color from black to yellowish-green with irregular yellowish flecks and yellowish-white or black spines.
Host Plants: Mostly nettle, but also false nettle, pellitory and hops.

Red Admiral

White Admiral

Scientific Name: *Limentis arthemis.*
Wingspan: 2-1/2 to 3-5/8 inches.
Distinctive Markings: Black topwings with distinctive white bands that run across the middle on both sides.
Habitat: Areas with deciduous trees or mixed with evergreens, especially near forest edges and clearings.
Caterpillar: Mottled off-white, olive and greenish-yellow body with a bristled hump behind its head.
Host Plants: A variety of hardwood trees and shrubs, including birch, poplar, willow, black cherry and hawthorn.

White Admiral

Baltimore Checkerspot
Scientific Name: *Euphydryas phaeton.*
Wingspan: 1-5/8 to 2-1/2 inches.
Distinctive Markings: Black wings have orange- and cream-colored spots, plus orange crescents mark outer margins.
Habitat: Wet meadows and bogs; forest hillsides.
Caterpillar: Caterpillars are black with orange stripes and branching black spines.
Host Plants: Turtlehead, false foxglove, plantain and white ash tree.

Milbert's Tortoiseshell
Scientific Name: *Nymphalis milberti.*
Wingspan: 1-3/4 to 2 inches.
Distinctive Markings: Bright orange and yellow outer bands, with faint blue dots on the margins.
Habitat: Prefers higher altitudes, but can be found in all types of temperate habitats within its range.
Caterpillar: Black, spiny caterpillars have small white flecks, and a green and yellow stripe on each side.
Host Plant: Nettle.

Bronze Copper
Scientific Name: *Hyllolycaena hyllus.*
Wingspan: 1-1/4 to 1-3/8 inches.
Distinctive Markings: On males, tops of the forewings are dark copper-brown with an iridescent purple sheen. Females sport bright-orange to yellowish forewings with dark spots. Both have gray hindwings with orange edges.
Habitat: Near host plants in ditches, swamps, streams and other damp areas.
Caterpillar: Bright yellowish-green with a dark line running down the back.
Host Plants: Docks, particularly curly dock and knotweeds.

Meadow Fritillary
Scientific Name: *Boloria bellona.*
Wingspan: 1-1/4 to 1-7/8 inches.
Distinctive Markings: Reddish-orange wings with heavy black dashes and dots. This butterfly's squared-off angular forewings and its lack of silver markings distinguish it from other fritillaries.
Habitat: Moist meadows, hay fields, pastures, roadsides and bogs. They will also visit gardens.
Caterpillar: Purplish-black, sometimes mottled with yellow, with branching spines protruding from brown bumps.
Host Plant: Violet.

Great Spangled Fritillary

Scientific Name: *Speyeria cybele.*
Wingspan: 2-1/8 to 3 inches.
Distinctive Markings: Orange with black-patterned markings. Yellow band and silver spots on underside of hind wings.
Habitat: Open, moist-soiled meadows, woodlands, valleys and pastures.
Caterpillar: Black with black and orange spines. Caterpillars go dormant in winter and feed on violet leaves in spring.
Host Plant: Violet.

Aphrodite Fritillary

Scientific Name: *Speyeria aphrodite.*
Wingspan: 2 to 3 inches.
Distinctive Markings: Tawny-orange wings, accented with a splattering of dark spots, dashes and crescents. Underneath, the forewing is lighter with similar markings, except for a band of shiny silver spots along the edge. The hind wing sports a richer cinnamon hue and a multitude of silver spots that become more triangular away from the body.
Habitat: Wooded areas, tall-grass prairies, foothills and mountain meadows.
Caterpillar: Spiny brownish-black with black spines.
Host Plant: Violet.

Gulf Fritillary

Scientific Name: *Agraulis vanillae.*
Wingspan: 2-1/2 to 2-7/8 inches.
Distinctive Markings: The tawny undersides of the wings display a pattern of large, silvery markings.
Habitat: Gardens and sunny, open areas filled with flowers.
Caterpillar: Bright orange and covered in soft, black spines.
Host Plant: Passionflower.

Variegated Fritillary

Scientific Name: *Euptoieta claudia.*
Wingspan: 1-3/4 to 2-1/4 inches.
Distinctive Markings: Elongated, tawny-orange wings with dark zigzagged lines and black-dotted margins; hind wings are slightly scalloped and undersides of wings are mottled with whitish-brown patterns and splashes of orange.
Habitat: Commonly visits gardens and sunny open areas such as grasslands, fields, meadows, roadsides and mountaintops, but avoids deeply forested spaces.
Caterpillar: Salmon-red with bright-white stripes running the length of its body, rows of dark spines and knobby black horns at the head.
Host Plants: Passionflower, mayapple, flax, violets, pansies, purslane, stonecrop, moonseed and plantain.

Great Spangled Fritillary

Aphrodite Fritillary

Gulf Fritillary

Variegated Fritillary

Black Swallowtail
Scientific Name: *Papilio polyxenes.*
Wingspan: 3-1/8 to 4-1/2 inches.
Distinctive Markings: Black wings with two rows of light dots; blue markings and black-centered orange eyespots on hind wings; rows of yellow dots on abdomen.
Habitat: Open areas including gardens, fields and marshes.
Caterpillar: Bright green with black bands and yellow or orange dots.
Host Plants: Carrots, parsley, Queen Anne's lace and dill.

Anise Swallowtail
Scientific Name: *Papilio zeliacon.*
Wingspan: 2-5/8 to 3 inches.
Distinctive Markings: Wide, yellow bands across wings; blue marking and orange eyespots on hind wings.
Habitat: Prefers open fields, deserts, canyons, roadways and forest clearings.
Caterpillar: Green or greenish-blue with thick, black stripes and orange dots.
Host Plants: Anise, sweet fennel, parsley, carrots, cow parsnip, citrus trees and seaside angelica.

Giant Swallowtail
Scientific Name: *Papilio cresphontes.*
Wingspan: 3-3/8 to 6-1/4 inches.
Distinctive Markings: Bright, horizontal bands of yellow dashes divide the dark topwings. Additional yellow spots line the edges. The tops also have an orange spot flanked by blue that's close to the body on each side. The tail is large with yellow centers. Undersides of wings are mostly yellow with black veining and blue and yellow spots.
Habitat: Citrus groves, sunny and open areas, forest edges, roads, rivers, glades and gardens.
Caterpillar: Brown with mottled white patches over the middle and rear. Measures almost 2-1/2 inches long at maturity. When threatened, it will produce a pair of orange horns and emit a powerful scent to ward off predators.
Host Plants: Citrus trees, prickly ash, hopwood and rue.

Spicebush Swallowtail
Scientific Name: *Papilio troilus.*
Wingspan: 3-1/2 to 4-1/2 inches.
Distinctive Markings: Obsidian black wings. Males are greenish-blue on lower wings, females are a distinct blue on lower wings. Both have white dots along the edges and a pair of orange dots between the distinctive tails.
Habitat: Forest edges, meadows, gardens and fields.
Caterpillar: As it grows, the larva turns green and forms a set of rimmed orange eyespots on either side of the thorax.
Host Plants: Spice bush, sassafras, red bay and other bays.

Zebra Swallowtail

Scientific Name: *Eurytides marcellus.*
Wingspan: 2-3/8 to 3-1/2 inches.
Distinctive Markings: Triangle-shaped wings, long tails and white to greenish-blue wings with bold, black stripes. Hind wings have blue and red spots on top and a scarlet stripe on the undersides.
Habitat: Near water and in undeveloped areas such as woodlands, marshes and meadows.
Caterpillar: Young caterpillars are black with yellow and white bands. Older ones may be gray or black with yellow and white cross bands. They are larger at the front, tapering toward the rear and grow up to 1-1/2 inches long.
Host Plants: Pawpaws and related species.

Two-Tailed Swallowtail

Scientific Name: *Papilio multicaudata.*
Wingspan: 3-3/8 to 5-1/8 inches.
Distinctive Markings: One long and one medium-length tail on each hind wing; bright-blue patches on edges of hind wings.
Habitat: Canyons, mid-range mountains and gardens.
Caterpillar: Bright, apple-green caterpillars have a yellow hump and black-rimmed yellow eyespots. The caterpillar turns reddish-brown before it pupates.
Host Plants: Cherry, ash and common hoptree.

Eastern Tiger Swallowtail

Scientific Name: *Papilio glaucus.*
Wingspan: 3-1/2 to 6-1/2 inches.
Distinctive Markings: Black tiger-like stripes on yellow background (all males and some females) and distinctive swallow-like tails. Some females are black.
Habitat: Gardens, parks, orchards and woodlands, particularly near broadleaf trees and shrubs.
Caterpillar: Dark green with enlarged front and two prominent eyespots. Overwinters in a wood-like chrysalis.
Host Plants: Ash, aspen, basswood, birch, cherry, cottonwood, sweetbay, tulip and willow trees.

Western Tiger Swallowtail

Scientific Name: *Papilio rutulus.*
Wingspan: 2-5/8 to 4 inches.
Distinctive Markings: Black tiger-like stripes on yellow background (all males and some females) and distinctive swallow-like tails.
Habitat: Gardens, parks, orchards and woodlands, particularly near broadleaf trees and shrubs.
Caterpillar: Dark green with enlarged front and two prominent eyespots. Overwinters in a wood-like chrysalis.
Host Plants: Ash, aspen, basswood, birch, cherry, sweet bay, tulip, cottonwood and willow trees.

Zebra Swallowtail

Two-Tailed Swallowtail

Eastern Tiger Swallowtail

Western Tiger Swallowtail

Eastern Comma

Question Mark

Pearl Crescent

Silver-Spotted Skipper

Eastern Comma
Scientific Name: *Polygonia comma.*
Wingspan: 1-3/4 to 2-1/2 inches.
Distinctive Markings: Silver or whitish comma shape on underside of hind wing. Rusty brown upper forewings with black splotches; upper hind wings feature a broad black margin with a short tail. Sharply angled wings.
Habitat: Deciduous woodlands near water.
Caterpillar: Light green to brown and about 1 inch long, with spines on body. Overwinters in a wood-like chrysalis.
Host Plants: All members of the elm and nettle families.

Question Mark
Scientific Name: *Polygonia interrogationis.*
Wingspan: 2-3/8 to 2-5/8 inches.
Distinctive Markings: Angular orange and brown-black wings with a silvery question mark on the undersides.
Habitat: Open woods, fields, parks, roadsides, orchards and sunny streamsides.
Caterpillar: Its blackish body is covered with white dots and yellow or orange lines, as well as bristle-like orange spines. The spines closest to the head are black. At maturity, it measures 1-5/8 inches.
Host Plants: Nettle, hops, hackberry and elm tree.

Pearl Crescent
Scientific Name: *Phyciodes tharos.*
Wingspan: 1 to 1-1/2 inches.
Distinctive Markings: Top of wings are a rich, golden orange with a patchwork of dark brown or black marks. Underneath, there is a pearl-colored crescent mark near each wing edge.
Habitat: Fields, meadows, gardens, roadsides and other open spaces.
Caterpillar: Pale brown with black head; brown branched spines and a white to yellow lateral stripe.
Host Plant: Aster.

Silver-Spotted Skipper
Scientific Name: *Epargyreus clarus.*
Wingspan: 1-3/4 to 2-5/8 inches.
Distinctive Markings: Elongated, brownish-black wings marked with glassy yellowish-gold, squared-off spots on upper forewings, and silvery-white patches and metallic silver margins on undersides of lobed hind wings.
Habitat: Commonly visits gardens, woodlands, waterways, roadsides, parks and meadows.
Caterpillar: Growing to 2 inches long, the larvae boast light-yellow-and-green striped, spindle-shaped bodies and large, reddish-brown heads with two orange eyespots.
Host Plants: Woody legumes, including mossy locust, black locust, false indigo, hog-peanut, American potato-bean, common honeylocust and wisteria.

Spring Azure

Scientific Name: *Celastrina ladon.*

Wingspan: 3/4 to 1-1/4 inches.

Distinctive Markings: The wings of adult males are a silvery violet blue from above, and grayish white with black markings and outer edges from below. Females are duller in color with more white and a broad black border on the topside.

Habitat: Open roadsides, clearings, forested areas and brushy fields.

Caterpillar: Colors vary from cream to yellow-green and pink to brown. They are often marked with darker patterns on the back and sides.

Host Plant: Flowering dogwood—they eat the flowers rather than the leaves because they are more nutritious.

Spring Azure

Common Wood Nymph

Scientific Name: *Cercyonis pegala.*

Wingspan: 1-7/8 to 3 inches.

Distinctive Markings: Light to dark cocoa wings on top with two large eyespots amid a splash of yellow or lighter brown on both the top and bottom sides of forewing. The lower part of each wing also bears one to three eyespots on top, and up to six eyespots underneath.

Habitat: Open oak, pine and mixed woodlands, meadows, prairies, bogs, along slow rivers and streams with overhanging vegetation, thickets and grassy roadsides.

Caterpillar: Yellow-green and furry with alternating dark and light stripes running the length of its body.

Host Plants: Purpletop and other grasses.

Common Wood Nymph

Orange Sulphur

Scientific Name: *Colias eurytheme.*

Wingspan: 1-1/2 to 2-3/8 inches.

Distinctive Markings: There is always some orange present, whether it's the hue of the wings or splotches on the top or underside of the hind wings.

Habitat: Open spaces such as fields, prairies and yards.

Caterpillar: Small, grass-green caterpillar is covered with tiny, white hairs. White stripes edged in black run along its side. May have pink stripes below the white ones.

Host Plants: Legumes, alfalfa, clover, vetch and senna.

Orange Sulphur

Cabbage White

Scientific Name: *Pieris rapae.*

Wingspan: 1-1/2 to 2 inches.

Distinctive Markings: White forewings with dark tips. Males also bear a single black spot on each forewing, and females have two dark spots. Undersides are yellow- or gray-green.

Habitat: Gardens, fields, roadsides and areas near streams.

Caterpillar: Bright green with a thin yellow line down its back and yellow dashes on the body. It's covered in short, soft hairs that appear fuzzy.

Host Plants: Cabbage, broccoli, collards, radishes, pepper grass, nasturtiums and mustard plants.

Cabbage White

BIRDS&BLOOMS

GARDENING

for birds & butterflies

Index

A

Abelia 73
Admiral 37
red 46, 86, 150, 183
white 75, 99, 183
Agastache 58, 61, 67
Alder 31
common 35
Allium 33
Alyssum
golden 61
sweet 58, 76, 78, 79
Anemone, Japanese 108, 113
Angel's trumpet 61
Anise hyssop 78
Apple 75, 181
Arborvitae, eastern 141, 147
Artemisia 183
Powis Castle 15
Ash 98, 122, 187
white 184
Aspen 181, 187
Aster 19, 29, 61, 78, 98, 107, 189
New England 13
smooth 13
Azalea 61
pinkshell 36
pinxterbloom 48
Azure, spring 46, 189

B

Bachelor's button 67
Backyard certification programs 21
Baptisia 67
Barberry 10, 140
Bats 61, 91
Bean, scarlet runner 14, 75
Bearberry, common 140
Beardtongue, large-flowered 13
Beautyberry 140
Bees 61
bumble 64
honeybee 64
leafcutter 64
virescent green metallic 64
Bee balm 61, 64, 67
Beech 31
Beetle
milkweed leaf 64
Pennsylvania leatherwing 64
red milkweed 64
Bergenia 39, 43
Berry-producing plants, landscaping with 10, 14, 102-103, 121
Birch 31, 182, 183, 187
Bird food 160-179
(also see Birdseed)
caterpillars 10
fruit 45, 136
insects 10
mealworms 45, 51, 59, 84, 136
peanut butter 136
Birdbath 11, 45, 59, 85, 103, 118, 136
heated 119, 133, 149
Birdhouse 27, 45, 50-51, 137
dimensions 45
cleaning 27, 137
Birdseed 170-189
(also see Bird food)
make your own mix 111
millet 119, 133
natural 85
no-mess 84
nyjer 44, 59, 119
safflower 27
sunflower 119, 136
Bittersweet, American 143
Blackbird, red-winged 177
Black-eyed Susan 61, 107
sweet 13
Blanket flower 31, 58, 61, 67
Blazing star 29, 67, 98
dense 13
dotted 13
prairie 13
Bleeding heart 33
Blue butterflies 34, 37
cassius 29
eastern tailed 29
silvery 46
tailed 86
Blue spirea 26, 61, 73
Blueberry 75
Bluebirds 26, 27, 45, 103, 118, 133, 161
eastern 161
mountain 161
western 161
Boxwood 140
Broccoli 75, 78, 189
Buckeye butterflies 86
common 71, 99, 182
Buckeye, red 37
Bugleweed 58, 115
common 33
Bully birds, deterring 27
Buntings 118
indigo 178
lazuli 178
snow 100, 103
Burning bush 112
Butterflies
(also see Host plants)
hibernation 99, 120
life cycle of 86
overwintering 120
Butterfly box 48, 99
Butterfly bush 29, 61, 73, 77
dwarf 78
Butterfly gardening 22-23, 26, 28-29, 32-37, 38-39, 60-61, 66-75, 99, 106-111, 112-113
Butterfly weed 13, 68
Buttonbush 73

C

Calibrachoa 19, 42, 68, 80, 81, 82, 114, 115
California lilac 77
Camellia 140
Campanula 61
Candytuft 41, 61
Canna 61
Cardinal flower 13, 68, 98
Cardinal, northern 10, 27, 45, 103, 118, 122, 135, 169
Carrot 27, 75, 186
Cassia 29
Catbird, gray 10, 122, 176
Catchfly, royal 13
Catmint 77
Celosia 107
Checkerspot, Baltimore 184
Cherry 181, 187
wild black 37, 183
Chickadees 10, 27, 36, 44, 133
black-capped 118, 175
Carolina 48
Chokeberry, black 110
Chokecherry, common 35
Christmas tree 133
Chrysanthemum 41, 98, 107, 112
Clematis 31, 111
golden 113
Cleome 68
Columbine 33, 38, 61
Comma butterflies 120, 150
eastern 188
Coneflower 29, 61, 64, 78, 107, 145
pale purple 13
purple 13
Container gardens for wildlife 19, 40-43, 80-83, 114-117, 146-147
Copper, bronze 184
Coral bells 40, 68, 77, 114
Coralberry 141
Coreopsis 68
Cosmos 68
Cotoneaster 98, 141
Cottonwood 31, 187
Crabapple 10, 121, 122
Creeper, brown 133
Crescent, pearl 86, 188
Cricket, snowy tree 65
Crocosmia 68
Crocus 61
Crossbill 148
red 179
Culver's root 13

D

Dahlia 107
Daisy, gloriosa, dwarf 113
Daylily 77
Deadheading 14, 58, 119
Dianthus 39
Dill 27, 75, 186
Dogwood 10, 122, 141
flowering 35, 38, 98, 189
redosier 145
Dove, mourning 84, 163
Dragonflies 103
green darner 63
twelve-spotted skimmer 63
widow skimmer 63
Drivable gardens 14
Duskywing butterflies
columbine 33
sleepy 46

E

Elderberry 110
Elfin butterflies 141
frosted 46
Henry's 142
Elm 182, 188
American 31
Emperor, hackberry 182
English daisy 43
Evergreens, landscaping with 14, 103, 137, 140-143, 144-145

F

False aster 108
False cypress 145
False indigo 13, 188
Feather reed grass 139
Feeders
bird 27, 53, 85, 124-125, 126, 136, 156, 157
butterfly 59
ground tray 85, 118
hopper-style 99
orange 27, 45, 52
peanut 133, 149
suet 27, 45, 99, 119, 133, 136, 148
sugar water 44, 59, 92, 99, 127
tube 99
Felicia daisy 117
Fennel 27, 75
bronze 78, 79
sweet 186
Fern 38
Fertilizer 19
Finches 37, 45
house 27, 44, 118, 176
purple 176
Fireflies 87
Firethorn 141
Flicker, northern 170
Floating plants 93
Floss flower 19, 69, 78, 79, 81, 82
Flowering tobacco 69
Flies 61
bee 65
flower 65
long-legged 65
Foamflower 43
Forget-me-not 33
Fothergilla 35
Fountain grass 108
Fountains, landscaping with 14, 45
Foxglove 34
Fringe tree 73
Fritillary butterflies 46, 141
Aphrodite 185
great spangled 86, 185
gulf 185
meadow 184
variegated 29, 185
Fruit trees, landscaping with 11
Fuchsia 19, 69

G

Garden care
fall 14, 98, 114
spring 9, 26
summer 58
winter 132, 133
Gentian, bottle 13
Gladiolus 61
Globe thistle 69, 77
Goldenrod 64, 108, 112
Ohio 13
showy 13
stiff 13
Goldfinch, American 44, 58, 99, 119, 135, 176
Gooseberry 152
Grape 111
Grape hyacinth 61
Grapeholly, Oregon 113
Grass, ornamental 31
Grosbeak 27, 37, 45
black-headed 162
evening 162
pine 162
rose-breasted 10, 11, 162

H

Hackberry 182, 188
Hairstreak 36, 37, 46, 70
coral 110
great purple 88

Hawthorn..... 15, 110, 122, 181, 183
Heath, winter 139
Heavenly bamboo 146
   dwarf 113
Hedges 10
Heliotrope 69, 81
Hemlock 142
Hibiscus 19, 73
Holly, yellow 147
Hollyhock 70
Honeysuckle 31
   scarlet 61
   trumpet 74, 76, 87
Hops.............................183, 188
Host plants........10, 23, 27, 29,
   46, 180-189
Hosta 38
Hummingbirds 30-31, 37, 44,
   84, 99, 118
   Allen's.............................31
   Anna's 31, 166
   black-chinned 31, 118, 166
   blue-throated 31
   broad-billed.........................31
   broad-tailed 31, 118
   calliope.............................31
   Costa's.............................31
   gardening for 16-19, 31, 32-37,
   38-39, 60-61, 66-75,
   76-79, 106-111, 112-113
   hand-feeding.........................127
   magnificent.........................31
   ruby-throated 31, 118, 166
   rufous.................... 31, 118, 166
Hyacinth 61

I
Impatiens 70
Incense-cedar........................147
Insects, beneficial 58, 62-65, 103
Ironweed...................... 183
   New York 70
   tall 13
Ironwood...........................31
Irruption.....................133, 148
Ivy, Boston.........................111

J
Jays..............................44, 133
   blue 177
   Steller's..........................177
   western scrub.........................177
Joe Pye weed......................64, 108
   tall 13
Johnny-jump-up...................... 29, 139
Junco, dark-eyed........... 9, 99, 103,
   119, 148, 173
Juniper...........................142, 147
   creeping 146
   golden 146, 147

Holger....................147
Juvenile birds............... 59, 84, 152

K
Katydid, broad-winged 65
Kinglets 45
   ruby-crowned 179
Knotweed 113, 184

L
Lacewing, green.......................65
Lady butterflies
   American 183
   painted.............46, 70, 150, 183
Lamb's ear 31
Landscaping for wildlife 9-11, 12,
   14-15, 48, 100-103, 119, 132
Lantana............... 15, 19, 70, 78, 183
Lark, horned 165
Lavender 58, 61, 70, 76
Leadplant 13
Leadwort 116
Licorice plant....................81, 116
Lilac 29, 36, 41
   French 39
Lily...................................61
Linden 110
Lobelia 42, 81, 83
Locust 15
Longwing, zebra.......................88
Lungwort 34, 38
Lupine 34
   wild 13

M
Mahonia 142
Maiden grass..................... 112, 145
Mallow, rose 13
Maple 31, 104-105
   bigleaf 110
   Japanese 113
   paperbark.............................145
Marble butterflies 46
Marguerite daisy 42, 114
Marigold...........................61, 79
   Mexican mint 15
Martin, purple..........................167
Meadowlarks
   eastern 165
   western 165
Mexican feather grass 117
Mexican sunflower 108
Migration
   bird................... 10, 45, 59, 99,
   100-103, 118
   butterfly.......46, 103, 120, 181
Milkweed 29, 64
   showy 71
   swamp.......................72, 78
Mint..................................29

Miscanthus...................................139
Mockingbird, northern.................163
Mockorange..........................36
Monarch 23, 29, 46, 68,
   86, 150, 181
   migration 120
   overwintering 151
Monarch Watch, University
   of Kansas 23
Monkey flower..........................152
Moonflower..........................61
Moths..................................61
Mountain ash 142
   European 121
   Korean 121
Mourning cloak ...105, 120, 133, 182
Mulberry 31

N
Nasturtium 29, 70, 76, 189
Native plants 10, 12-13, 14-15,
   102-103, 136
   for dry soil.........................13
   for medium soil.........................13
   for moist soil.........................13
   locating 20, 103
Nectar 14, 29, 58
Nests..................................59
   boxes for 137, 152
   hummingbird...................... 30-31
   materials for 27, 31
Nettle 183, 184, 188
New Jersey tea 36
Nighthawk, common 88
Nodding pink onion 13
Nuthatches..................36, 44, 119
   red-breasted..........................168
   white-breasted..........................168

O
Ocotillo 61
Orangetip butterflies......................46
Oregano 78
Orioles........10, 27, 44, 52, 118, 172
   Baltimore..........................172
   Bullock's..........................172
   orchard..........................172
Osteospermum......................77, 115
Owens-Pike, Douglas 15
Owls
   attracting..........................88
   eastern screech..........................165
   great horned..........................165
   western screech 165

P
Pampas grass, dwarf.................113
Pansy 29, 34, 41, 185
Parsley 27, 75, 79, 186
Pasque flower 31

Passionflower 74, 185
Paulownia, royal..........................47
Pear..................................75
Penick, Pam..........................15
Penstemon 71, 77
   bush 152
Pentas 19, 71
Perennial sunflower 80
Pest control 15, 26
   organic 11, 59
Petunia 61, 82, 116
Phlox 29
   creeping 33
   garden..........................69
   marsh..........................13
Phoebe, eastern 175
Pincushion flower..........................71
Pine
   mugo, dwarf..........................39
   eastern white..........................141
Pinkroot..........................34
Pipevine..........................29
Poplar.....................31, 181, 183
Potentilla 74
Prairie clover, purple 13
Prairie smoke 13
Primrose, evening..........................61
Projects
   bat house 90-91
   bird feeder.............124-125, 126
   birdseed ornaments 156
   bluebird house...................... 50-51
   cup and saucer feeder.............53
   frame bird feeder...................157
   hummingbird feeder......... 92, 127
   mini water garden 93
   oriole wreath.........................52
   peanut butter log...................156
   plantable gift tags.......... 154-155

Q
Quail, attracting..........................152
Queen butterfly........... 68, 181
Queen of the prairie...................13
Question mark................... 120, 188
Quince, flowering 10, 113
Quinine, wild 13

R
Rattlesnake master 13
Redbud........................... 10, 36, 98
Red-hot poker 71, 113
Red-spotted purple
   (see Admiral, white)
Redpoll, common......................173
Rhododendron.................. 10, 38, 61
Roberts, Deborah......................15
Robin, American 9, 45, 118, 122,
   133, 151, 163
Rock cress........................... 34, 43

Rose...........................10, 76
   rugosa..........................142
Rose of Sharon.................. 26, 83
Rosemary..........................15
Russian sage..........................61

S
Sage
   autumn 15, 110
   golden leaf.........................42, 81
   meadow..........................77
   Mexican bush 108
   pitcher..........................152
   tricolor..........................116
Salvia 61, 71
Sapsuckers 47
Sassafras..........................37
Satyrs...................... 46, 86, 140
   red-bordered..........................120
Sedum........................ 78, 109, 115,
   145, 182, 185
Senna, tree..........................29
Serviceberry 74, 121
Shooting star..........................13
Silk moth, giant..........................105
Siskin, pine..........................173
Sister, California..........................99
Skipper butterflies 36, 37, 46,
   70, 86, 140
   cloudywing..........................29
   common checkered 122
   fiery 120
   Leonard's 120
   silver-spotted......................... 188
Snapdragon 71, 182
Sneezeweed 112
Sparrows 9, 59, 118, 119
   American tree 174
   chipping..........................174
   song 174
   white-throated 174
Sphinx moths 73
   Pandora..........................111
   trumpet vine 74
Spice bush 37
Spruce..........................10
   Colorado blue 140, 145, 147
Squirrels, deterring..................27, 99
Stokes' aster 71
Stopover habitat 14, 100-103
Strawberry..........................75
Suet 27, 45, 99, 119,
   133, 136, 148
Sulphur butterflies 29, 34,
   37, 46, 86
   cloudless 29, 120
   orange 189
   orange-barred..........................29
Sumac..........................110
Summersweet 26, 74

Sunflower 61, 109	scarlet 178
Swallow, tree 167	western 178
Swallowtail butterflies..... 29, 58, 105	Thistle 29, 58, 183
anise 186	Thrush, wood...............................163
black 27, 75, 186	Thyme, creeping 39, 58
eastern black...........................75	Titmouse, tufted 27, 133, 173
eastern tiger 37, 88, 187	Tortoiseshell butterflies 120, 150
giant 186	Milbert's 184
pipevine...................................29	Towhees....................................9
spicebush.....................37, 186	eastern 170
two-tailed.........................187	rufous-sided 170
western tiger.................110, 187	spotted...................................170
zebra 46, 187	Trumpet vine.....................61, 74, 87
Sweet William 72	Tulip tree 37, 187
Sweet, Rebecca..........................15	Turk's cap 121
Swift, chimney 167	Turtlehead 109, 187
Switchgrass......................... 12, 139	
bitter 145	**V**
	Verbena.................... 19, 72, 78, 79,
T	81, 116, 117, 182
Tanagers............ 10, 27, 44, 45, 118	Veronica 58, 72

Vervain, purpletop................ 78, 109	common 189
Viburnum............................ 98, 110	Wood spurge 40, 43
American cranberrybush 122	Woodpeckers.................44, 45, 133
Viceroy butterflies................. 99, 181	attracting.............................. 122
Viola 29, 34, 40	downy 171
Violet 29	hairy 170
bird's-foot 13	pileated 171
Virginia creeper...........................111	red-bellied 171
	red-headed 152, 171
W	Wrens................................... 10, 118
Wallflower 40, 41	Carolina 168
Warblers.................. 10, 45, 59, 118	house 168
prothonotary 164	
yellow 164	**Y**
yellow-rumped.......................164	Yarrow 29, 58, 72, 77
Waxwings	Yellow coneflower 13
Bohemian 179	Yellowthroat, common 164
cedar............................ 122, 179	Yucca 74
Weed control 11, 12	
Weigela..37	**Z**
Whip-poor-will 167	Zinnia 29, 58, 72, 78, 79, 117

White butterflies	
cabbage 34, 75, 189	
spring 46	
West Virginia..........................46	
Wild hyacinth 13	
Wildlife gardens	
designing.................. 9-11, 14-15	
fall 100-103, 106-113	
shade 12, 38	
small-space 14	
spring 32-39	
summer..............................66-79	
urban.......................................14	
winter 138-145	
Willow 31, 181, 182, 183, 187	
pussy.......................................36	
Winterberry.................... 142, 145	
Wishbone flower 82	
Wisteria.................................37, 188	
Witch hazel 31, 113, 143, 145	
Wood nymph butterflies 29	

what's your zone?

Find out which plants will thrive in your area.

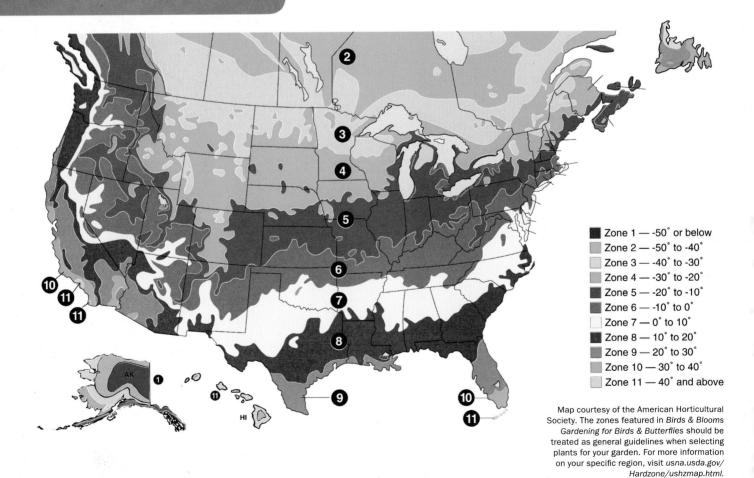

■	Zone 1 — -50˚ or below
■	Zone 2 — -50˚ to -40˚
■	Zone 3 — -40˚ to -30˚
■	Zone 4 — -30˚ to -20˚
■	Zone 5 — -20˚ to -10˚
■	Zone 6 — -10˚ to 0˚
□	Zone 7 — 0˚ to 10˚
■	Zone 8 — 10˚ to 20˚
■	Zone 9 — 20˚ to 30˚
■	Zone 10 — 30˚ to 40˚
■	Zone 11 — 40˚ and above

Map courtesy of the American Horticultural Society. The zones featured in *Birds & Blooms Gardening for Birds & Butterflies* should be treated as general guidelines when selecting plants for your garden. For more information on your specific region, visit *usna.usda.gov/ Hardzone/ushzmap.html.*